Praise for Mark Di Vincenzo and
Buy Ketchup in May and

"The breezy little paperback offers hundreds of tips from the former
investigative reporter, whose research is evident and
sources carefully listed at the end. That keeps the attribution
from cluttering up the info, which ranges from sublime to silly."
—*Los Angeles Times* travel blog

"Well worth checking out."
—*Dayton Daily News*

"Food for thought."
—*Boston Globe*

"Sure to liven up a boring cocktail party. . . .
[W]ill enlighten, surprise, even disappoint you."
—*Houston Chronicle*

"Straightforward."
—*Richmond Times-Dispatch*

"Full of amusing and helpful timing tips."
—*Sacramento Bee*

"Strangely compelling."
—*Guardian* (UK)

"[Di Vincenzo] doles out advice with practical reasoning. . . .
[U]seful and interesting."
—*Plain Dealer* (Cleveland)

"[Di Vincenzo] gets into the nitty-gritty of why timing really is everything."
—*Chicago Tribune*

BUY SHOES ON WEDNESDAY AND TWEET AT 4:00

Also by Mark Di Vincenzo

Buy Ketchup in May and Fly at Noon:
A Guide to the Best Time to Buy This, Do That and Go There

Your Pinkie Is More Powerful Than Your Thumb:
And 333 Other Surprising Facts That Will Make You Wealthier,
Healthier and Smarter Than Everyone Else

BUY SHOES ON WEDNESDAY AND TWEET AT 4:00

More of the Best Times to Buy This, Do That and Go There

MARK DI VINCENZO

WILLIAM MORROW
An Imprint of HarperCollinsPublishers

HarperCollins books may be purchased for educational, business, or sales promotional use. For information please write: Special Markets Department, HarperCollins Publishers, 10 East 53rd Street, New York, NY 10022.

FIRST EDITION

Based on the design by Justin Dodd

Library of Congress Cataloging-in-Publication Data has been applied for.

ISBN 978-0-06-211770-0

12 13 14 15 16   OV/RRD   10 9 8 7 6 5 4 3 2 1

FOR FRED AND TONI DI VINCENZO

CONTENTS

Acknowledgments xi

Introduction xiii

1 Getting It 1

2 Getting Rid of It 17

3 Getting Things Done 29

4 Getting Around 45

5 Getting Pretty 57

6 Getting Rich 67

7 Getting Healthy 81

8 Getting the Job Done 105

9 Around the House 119

10 Around the World 131

11 Around the Kitchen 147

12 Around the Yard 155

13 Around the Kennel 165

14 Around the Playground 175

Sources 185

Index 211

ACKNOWLEDGMENTS

This book is crammed with tips and advice from dozens of experts, and I'd like to thank them here collectively for all of the great information they provided.

I also owe a debt to Kate Nintzel, my editor, for all the big and little things she did to make this book interesting and useful, and to Michelle Wolfson, my agent, for her encouragement, her business smarts and her tweets.

As always, thanks to Jayne, my incredible wife, for her patience, wisdom and love.

INTRODUCTION

Let me get this confession out of the way in the first sentence: I didn't think I could write this book.

After *Buy Ketchup in May and Fly at Noon: A Guide to the Best Time to Buy This, Do That and Go There* was released, readers asked me if I planned to write a follow-up. I said no, forget about it, it's not going to happen. Then, a few months later, they went from asking me to do it to urging me to do it. I didn't want to even consider it, but I knew why they became so insistent. *Buy Ketchup,* which I initially thought might not even attract an agent let alone a publisher, became very popular very quickly. Readers devoured the book's best-time tips, and soon after the release date in the fall of 2009, I promoted it on *Rachael Ray, All Things Considered* and other national TV and radio shows. *Entertainment Weekly* placed the book on its coveted back-cover Bullseye feature, and *Buy Ketchup* landed on the

New York Times best-seller list for several weeks toward the end of 2009. Glossy magazines and large and small newspapers from coast to coast reviewed it or reprinted information from it. Interview requests from as far away as Australia poured in well into 2010 and continued into 2011, and during those years, the book was also published in Russian, Italian, Turkish and Japanese.

So why not write a second edition and try to hit it big again?

Buy Ketchup ended up being about 175 pages long, but it could have been at least 500. I edited a ton of information down to a relatively slim book because I wanted everything in it—and I mean everything—to be of interest to the masses. If I removed a tip from the book during the editing process, I did it because I didn't think the housewife in Des Moines or the lawyer in Atlanta would find it relevant or interesting. *Buy Ketchup*'s success made me think I made the right choices to keep what I kept and omit what I omitted. In my mind, all the best and most relevant timing tips were in *Buy Ketchup,* so a second edition couldn't possibly offer readers enough of what they loved about the first book.

I was wrong. Very wrong.

After brainstorming with some smart people who saw great potential in a second edition, I went to work and discovered that there was much more material with widespread appeal and that this book could give readers hundreds more great tips about the best time to buy and do things and go places. I want you to know that this book contains none of the information that I deemed unworthy to be in *Buy Ketchup.*

This book and *Buy Ketchup* do have at least two very important things in common. First, the information in both books comes from experts, whether they're doctors and lawyers or mechanics and plumbers. Second, both books cover topics that the vast majority of us care a lot about—everything from money and health to travel and food. Of course, both books also include lots of tips on the best time to buy and do a wide range of things that will help you save more money, make more money and make better use of your time.

If you're familiar with *Buy Ketchup*, you'll notice that this book is different in some pretty obvious ways. For one thing, this book has fourteen chapters—seven more than in the first edition. Because it has twice as many chapters, it includes an even wider range of topics and subjects, such as whole sections on beauty tips, pets, cars and children as well as lots of information on the best times to get rid of things, such as perishable food, medicine and other things we may no longer want.

As I write this, I realize another difference is that this time—because there is so much I wasn't able to cover in this book—I know there probably is a third and maybe even a fourth edition to write. So stay tuned.

BUY SHOES ON WEDNESDAY AND TWEET AT 4:00

CHAPTER ONE

GETTING IT

About twenty-five years ago, I clipped a front-page graphic in *USA Today* about the best months of the year to buy furniture, kitchen appliances and other big-ticket items. I stuck it under a refrigerator magnet, referring to it, oh, about fifty times a year until it turned too yellow and faded for me to decipher anything from it. Knowing when to buy things has always been an interest of mine. If you can save a few bucks—or a few hundred bucks—by knowing when to make a purchase, why wouldn't you do it? The buying chapter in *Buy Ketchup in May and Fly at Noon* is arguably that book's most popular chapter, so it only makes sense to lead off this book with a chapter devoted to tips on the best time to buy things. In the following pages, you'll learn the best time to buy everything from TVs, textbooks and timeshares—don't do it!—to the best time to upgrade your computer.

WHICH IS THE BEST MONTH TO BUY A HIGH-DEFINITION TV? December is a great month to buy a lot of things, TVs included. But during years when TVs don't sell well in December, look for excellent postholiday sales, which stretch into the first half of January. Sales leading up to the Super Bowl in early February are very rarely super, despite common assumptions. Think about it: Why would retailers offer great deals when the demand is high? Do you see great prices on jewelry right before Valentine's Day? Any "Super Bowl TV Sales" you see in late January and early February typically come after retailers jack up the regular prices. **Second opinion:** Sales for older-model HDTVs can be very good in March and April. Electronics, including TVs, often go on sale then, when Japanese manufacturers release new models and retailers cut prices on older models.

WHICH IS THE BEST DAY OF THE WEEK TO BUY THINGS ONLINE? ShopItToMe.com, which tracks online sales from more than a hundred retailers, came up with this list:

MONDAYS: Men's and women's dress pants, on which shoppers can save nearly 50 percent. They can save more than that—about 55 percent—buying sunglasses.
TUESDAYS: Men's apparel. Expect to save more than 40 percent.
WEDNESDAYS: Shoes and children's clothes. Shoppers save about 40 percent on both.
THURSDAYS: Women's handbags. The average discount is 36 percent.
FRIDAYS: Jewelry, belts and scarves. The average discount is 42 percent.
SATURDAYS: Lingerie (37 percent off) and jackets/outerwear (51 percent off).
SUNDAYS: Swimsuits (52 percent off).

OTHER THAN BLACK FRIDAY AND CYBER MONDAY, WHICH ARE THE BEST DAYS OF THE YEAR TO SHOP ONLINE FOR CHRISTMAS GIFTS? Many retailers offer early "Black Friday" sales on the weekends before and after Halloween. Another good time is the three or four days before

Christmas. If you see something you want around Halloween, expect discounts of about 30 percent. If the discounts aren't at least 20 percent, wait—you'll probably find what you want cheaper later or on another site. As for the days before Christmas, be careful. Some websites do offer great deals, especially during seasons when sales are sluggish, but some hope to take advantage of procrastinators. Also keep in mind that your savings might get wiped out by overnight or express shipping.

WHICH IS THE BEST MONTH TO BUY A CELL PHONE? June or December. June because of high school graduations and December because of Christmas and Hanukkah. Stores often offer the best deals of the year during these two months as they engage in a fierce competition for sales. June wasn't always a big month for cell-phone sales, but parents whose children work summer jobs or are leaving home for college in August want to be able to reach them, so they buy then. And cell phones have become common holiday gifts. **A second opinion:** February. Watch for buy-one-get-one-free sales around Valentine's Day so you can buy a phone for yourself and one for your sweetie. **Money-saving tip:** When phone stores are experiencing a slow month, sometimes they'll waive activation fees or offer instant rebates to buyers. Look for these incentives during the last week of the month.

WHEN IS THE BEST TIME TO BUY AN IPAD? Find out when Apple plans to release the next latest and greatest model, and if that release date is in six months or less, wait. If history is any indication, the newer model will be thinner and faster, offer a longer battery life and a better screen and cost about the same—or even a bit less. Apple has done the same thing with its iPods and iPhones, releasing sleeker and better next-generation models for often less money. **Money-saving tip:** New iPads rarely go on sale, but you can buy refurbished models from Apple for $120 to $170 less than the regular price, depending on how much memory you want.

WHEN IS THE BEST TIME TO NEGOTIATE A BETTER DEAL ON YOUR PHONE AND CABLE SERVICE? After you've been a customer for at least a year. That level of commitment will make the phone or cable service provider more likely to give you a better deal—or at least tell you about a better deal. Before you call, know how long you've been a customer, how much you pay per month and what deals, if any, the company is advertising on its website. After you give them your information, ask for any available discounts. If the person you're speaking with offers you no discounts, ask about any discounts you saw online or ask to speak with the supervisor. If that gets you nowhere, ask to be transferred to the cancellation department, where employees are more motivated—and sometimes have a financial incentive—to keep your business. **A final tip:** When it comes to your phone bill, go to BillShrink.com, a site that will ask you for your usage habits and then tell you about plans or carriers that can save you a lot of money. And it's a free service.

WHEN IS THE BEST TIME OF THE YEAR TO BUY A GYM MEMBERSHIP AND START USING IT? Summer. Most of the folks who made New Year's resolutions to work out abandoned them by the spring, and lots of people would rather exercise outdoors while the weather is nice. So not only is there less competition for weights and exercise equipment in gyms in the summer, but this is the time of year when gyms will waive sign-up fees and give away a free month to entice new members.

WHICH IS THE BEST TIME OF DAY AND DAY OF THE WEEK TO SHOP AT A WAREHOUSE STORE? Tuesday or Wednesday, when the store opens. The only line you'll see is the short one you'll be in before the doors open. Some stores will open as much as fifteen minutes early if they're ready for customers, so go early just in case, and even if the store doesn't open early, you'll get a great parking space. **The worst time and day?** 11 a.m. to 2 p.m. This is the most crowded time of the day because lunch-hour shoppers are there, as are the shoppers who go then because they know this is when stores offer the most free samples. So it's harder to get in and out quickly if you don't intend to linger. Saturdays and Sundays are the busiest days, but if you have to go on a weekend, try the hour before the store closes, when shoppers tend to thin out.

WHICH IS THE BEST MONTH TO BUY CLOTHES? January or May, if you want to save a lot of money. January's post-Christmas sales offer the best prices of the year, and you'll find great sales on spring-season clothes on the days leading up to Memorial Day. The downside is the selection, which won't be great either of those times because the clothes have been picked over. Department stores also discount socks, underwear and shoes in August, during pre-fall sales.

WHICH IS THE BEST MONTH TO BUY SUITS? Suits go on sale often, but January is a good month to count on. Not a lot of people buy suits then, so clothiers will lower prices to get you in their stores. **Tips:** Consider all-weather wool suits and timeless styles. And remember that you get what you pay for. You probably won't have a $100 suit in your closet four or five years from now, but you may have a $500 suit for ten years—or as long as you're able to fit into it.

WHEN IS THE BEST TIME OF THE YEAR TO BUY FANCY DRESSES FOR PROMS OR WEDDINGS? Winter. These dresses often arrive in stores in January. They won't be on sale then, but that's when you'll find the best selection, and buying in winter gives you plenty of time to get your dress altered. **How about wedding dresses?** December. Bridal shops bring in dresses in November, before Christmas and New Year's, when so many folks get engaged. If you shop for your dress in December, you'll beat the folks who just got engaged, and you'll be in a good position to negotiate with shop owners who want to boost their end-of-the-year sales.

WHICH IS THE BEST MONTH TO BUY PERFUME? January or March. Department stores and other retailers sell a lot of perfume at regular price in the days leading up to Christmas and Valentine's Day. You'll see decent sales after those holidays. Be smart and buy your Valentine's Day gift in January and your Mother's Day gift in March.

WHICH IS THE BEST MONTH TO BUY DEODORANT? May or June. In anticipation of the hot, sweaty summer months, manufacturers often distribute buy-one-get-one-free coupons and dollar-off coupons in May, with expiration dates at the end of June and sometimes the end of July. Stores very often discount deodorant at the same time, making for great opportunities to stock up for the year. **Tip:** Sometimes dollar-off coupons are good for any size deodorant, including travel or trial sizes. If that's the case, you can get deodorant for pocket change or for free if you shop at stores that double your coupons.

WHICH IS THE BEST MONTH TO BUY DIAMONDS IF YOU WANT THE BEST SELECTION? October. This is the beginning of a five-month period when jewelry stores have their largest inventories. That gives customers the greatest choice, and it's still at least a month before most folks start shopping for Christmas presents and engagement rings. Inventories shrink a lot by December, so if you wait till then, you'll have much less choice than you did in October. And brick-and-mortar stores often advertise sales between Christmas and New Year's to further reduce inventory for tax purposes, so by January there's even less to choose from.

WHICH IS THE BEST MONTH TO BUY DIAMONDS IF YOU WANT THE BEST PRICE? The summer. Sales are at their lowest of the year then, and jewelers have sales to move product. But be cautious: very often the diamonds for sale in those summer months are not a high quality. **Second opinion:** January. The Christmas rush is over, and that means you don't have to feel rushed, which you don't want when you're making such a large investment. **Did you know?** Jewelers often mark up diamonds so that they still make a hefty profit on stones sold during 50-percent-off sales.

WHICH IS THE BEST TIME OF DAY TO BUY JEWELRY? Late morning and late afternoon, assuming the store opens at 10 a.m. and closes at 8 p.m. First, let's summarize why jewelers say the other times aren't good: first thing in the morning, salespeople are drinking coffee, gabbing with coworkers and still cleaning glass cases and warming up gem-cleaning machines. In short, they're not yet focused on answering questions and selling. Jewelry stores, like other stores, are short staffed during the lunch hour, and customers often can't expect to have the undivided attention of a salesperson. The early afternoon is a sluggish time for nearly everyone, and the evening isn't good for customers because staffers want you out so they can close up and go home. In the late morning, 11 a.m. to noon, salespeople are freshest and are ready to help customers, and between 4 p.m. and 7 p.m., they've gotten their second wind and can give customers plenty of time. **What you can do:** When you buy a diamond, take your time. Learn everything you can about diamonds so you know what to look for. And get to know the salespeople. Customers who build a rapport with the salespeople and who know the most about diamonds get the best deals.

WHICH IS THE BEST MONTH TO BUY BROADWAY TICKETS? Broadway's slow months: January, February, September and October. This also has a lot to do with these four months being a relatively slow time for tourism in New York City. Less demand for tickets doesn't necessarily mean cheaper tickets, but it means they're easier to get. **Money-saving tip:** If you're buying tickets online, go to the websites for Playbill, TheaterMania and BroadwayBox and search for promotional codes, which can save you as much as half the price on the ticket. Major agencies, such as Ticketmaster and Telecharge, accept these codes, but you'll have to pay their high fees. You can avoid these fees if you buy at the theater box offices, and many theaters will let you use the coupon codes.

WHICH IS THE BEST MONTH TO BUY A GIFT CARD? January. Many of the people who don't want the gift cards they received for Christmas will sell them on websites such as eBay, giftcards.com and giftcardgranny.com, which sells them at 15 percent to 25 percent discounts. The best deals are in January, when most unwanted gift cards are for sale. **Second opinion:** November or December. Many restaurants and stores offer deals leading up to the end-of-the-year holidays. Start checking in November for deals that give you a $5 gift card if you buy a $25 gift card or a $10 gift card if you buy a $50 card.

WHICH IS THE BEST MONTH TO BUY CHRISTMAS CARDS? January. This is a no-brainer: stores want to get rid of the cards they didn't sell before Christmas. These cards tend to look the same year after year, so it's crazy to buy them in November and December. You'll see 50 percent discounts during the week after Christmas and deeper discounts than that after New Year's Day. **Tip:** Don't assume you'll find packages of Christmas cards at 99 percent off in February. By the middle of January, the vast majority of them are shipped back to warehouses and distribution centers.

WHICH IS THE BEST MONTH TO BUY CALENDARS? January and February. Calendar publishing companies make most of their money in October, November and December, hawking their products to businesses and to people who are looking for inexpensive Christmas and Hanukkah gifts. As soon as the ball drops at Times Square, calendars start losing their value, so stores often cut prices in half in January. Expect to pay 20 to 30 cents on the dollar by March and less than that as the year goes on, but by March selection is limited.

WHEN IS THE BEST TIME TO RENEW A MAGAZINE SUBSCRIPTION? Right before it expires. After you get notices that your subscription is about to expire, call—if you don't receive a call first—and explain that you don't want to pay the quoted price. Circulation for just about all magazines is dipping, and the magazines want to keep your business, not because they really need your $25 or $30 but because they need to show their advertisers that they have a healthy circulation so they can charge the advertisers more. Many magazines, *Consumer Reports* excluded, receive 80 percent of their revenue from advertisers, but they need lots of subscribers—even if those subscribers pay very little—to maintain the all-important advertising revenue.

WHEN IS THE BEST TIME TO BUY COLLEGE TEXTBOOKS? Right after the semester ends. Students who own them very often no longer need or want them and would like to get some money for them. And many students who need them for the next semester probably aren't thinking about buying books yet, so you won't have a lot of competition and sellers will be glad to get almost anything for books they don't want. This is true after the fall semester as well as after the spring semester, but you have to hustle more after the fall semester because there may be only four weeks before the spring semester begins and most students start thinking about their classes (and therefore books) for the new semester about two weeks before it begins. The key, of course, is knowing which classes you'll need to take the following semester far enough in advance and which books instructors plan to use. Students who know this have the upper hand and can buy $80 books for $20 or less right after one semester ends. As the next semester nears, those same books will sell for $50 or $60. **Second opinion:** After classes begin. If you wait, you may realize a friend is in your class, and you may be able to share the cost of the books. You also may discover that you may not actually need all the books your professor instructed you to buy. **E-books?** Electronic textbooks are not always cheaper, and the selection is not as good, but you *can* save big money by renting e-books, especially at a site called BigWords.com.

WHICH IS THE BEST MONTH TO BUY BACKPACKS? August. This is one of those purchases that fly in the face of logic. The demand is greatest for backpacks in August, so they should cost more then. But stores discount backpacks during back-to-school sales in August, and they can be hard to find after that, even at giant retailers such as Target and Walmart.

WHEN IS THE BEST TIME TO BUY TENTS, LANTERNS, SLEEPING BAGS AND OTHER CAMPING GEAR? Fall. After the peak camping season, stores often discount items that didn't sell as well as expected during the spring and summer. And stores sometimes will have sales to get people in the door, especially the weekend after Thanksgiving. The fall is also the time of year when campers most often sell their equipment and the selection of used stuff is best. When it gets cold, fewer campers think about selling their things and the selection isn't as good. As it warms up in spring, expect to pay full price at stores, and private sellers also aren't offering great deals. **Tip:** Garage sales tend to be the best places to find the best prices on camping gear.

WHEN IS THE BEST TIME TO UPGRADE YOUR COMPUTER? When your computer can no longer do what you need it to do and when you have the money to upgrade it. For example, you'll want to buy new hardware if the current hardware can't run the software you need it to run. There really is no better, specific answer, as there is for the best time to buy a new computer (during the back-to-school sales in August). **What you can do:** The components you might need to upgrade your computer don't typically go on sale at specific times of the year, but don't forget to do a good online search for what you need. You can save as much as 50 percent by finding the right site at the right time.

WHEN IS THE BEST TIME TO BUY PATIO FURNITURE? After Labor Day. This is especially true in the Northeast and Midwest but also in the South and West. Expect discounts of as much as 50 percent when it gets cooler and people spend less time outdoors and retailers look to make space in their stores.

WHICH IS THE BEST MONTH TO BUY A SWING SET? August or September. If you don't have one by then, you probably aren't going to buy one, and stores know that, so they lower prices to near cost this time of year. They want to get them out of their stores, and they'd rather they go into your pickup truck than into the 18-wheeler en route to a distribution center.

WHICH IS THE BEST MONTH TO BUY A POOL OR HOT TUB? December or January. How many people are seriously shopping for a pool or hot tub at a time when the whole Western world is shopping for Christmas and Hanukkah presents (in December) or trying to figure out how to pay off their holiday credit card bills (in January)? Practically no one. If you are, you'll have companies fighting for your business. Expect a great deal and great service, including free delivery and installation, especially if you make it clear to pool contractors that you're getting multiple estimates. The only trade-off is you can't use the pool right away. **A second opinion:** September. When most pool owners have closed or are closing their pools for the swimming season, you'll get a lot of attention and a great price if you're in the market for a pool. You'll also be first in line when pool companies start the excavating season for next summer's pools.

WHICH IS THE BEST MONTH TO BUY FLIP-FLOPS? August. Anyone who's inclined to wear flip-flops has theirs by August, when sales start to dip and prices drop. By October, it can be difficult to even find them in stores. **Did you know?** Late summer also is a good time to buy sunglasses. The best ones offer 100 percent ultraviolet-ray absorption.

WHICH IS THE BEST MONTH TO BUY A DEHUMIDIFIER? September. Humidity is more tolerable when it starts to cool down, and home improvement retailers don't want dehumidifiers taking up space in their stores during the winter months. So dehumidifiers go on sale in September.

WHICH IS THE BEST MONTH TO BUY CARPETING AND FLOORING? December or January. The busy time in this business is typically the fall for two reasons. Many people buy houses during the summer and spend a lot of money on them in the fall to get them looking the way they want. Others want to get their houses looking great in time for holiday get-togethers, so they're also spending in the fall. Business slows down dramatically by the middle of December and into January, when carpet stores typically offer their best deals of the year. If you have any money left over from the holiday shopping season, buy then.

WHEN IS THE BEST TIME TO BUY A MATTRESS AND BOX SPRING? Holiday weekends, especially Memorial Day and Presidents' Day. Some shoppers swear by May. Manufacturers often introduce their new models in June, so retailers will lower prices in May to make room for them. The truth is there is so much profit margin in mattresses and box springs that retailers frequently have sales, slashing prices by 30 percent and more and still making a hefty profit. **Money-saving tips:** (1) Don't be afraid to haggle. Because of the high profit margins, mattresses are one of the few products where you can shop like you're at a garage sale or a car dealership and negotiate with the store manager. (2) Small companies often sell excellent mattresses for a lot less. They spend less on advertisements and can afford to do that. (3) If you can't wait for a sale, check prices three or four weeks after you've bought. If you see your mattress on sale for a lower price, you may be able to negotiate a refund for the difference between what you paid and the sale price.

WHEN IS THE BEST TIME TO BUY A TIMESHARE? When you have money to burn. Crunch the numbers. It never makes sense, even if someone *gives* you a timeshare. You'll pull your hair out every time you receive a bill in the mail for the maintenance fees, which only go up over time. You'll want to sell your timeshare at some point because you won't want your heirs to inherit those maintenance fees. Good luck. You usually can't resell your timeshare for more than a few pennies on the dollar. And you can't write it off on your taxes, either. So if you have money to burn, go ahead and buy your timeshare.

WHEN IS THE BEST TIME OF THE MONTH TO CHECK FOR NEW COUPONS? The first of the month. The most serious coupon clippers know the first of the month is when many of the most serious coupon sites—coupons.com, redplum.com, thriftytiff.com and others—offer a new round of coupons.

WHEN IS THE BEST TIME OF DAY TO BUY PREPARED FOODS? About an hour before your grocery store closes. Many stores mark down prepared foods, such as rotisserie chicken and sushi, about an hour before closing if the food can't be sold the next day. Expect discounts of 50 percent on prepared foods. The same goes for bread and baked goods made in the store's bakery department.

CHAPTER TWO

GETTING RID OF IT

So now that you know the best time to buy a lot of different things, you might need to make room for the new stuff you want in your house. This chapter focuses on when to sell things you no longer want and when to throw away things that might make you sick if you keep them around too long, such as expired meat and cheese or medicine. After reading this chapter, you'll know the best day and month of the year to hold a garage sale; the best days to sell things online; the best month to sell stocks; the best time to sell gold; the best times to get rid of butter, sugar and salt; the best time to replace your toothbrush and much more.

WHICH IS THE BEST MONTH OF THE YEAR FOR A GARAGE SALE? April or May. This is largely because so many people have an expectation that there will be a lot of garage sales this time of year, and they're in the mood to go to these sales and make it a part of their weekend morning routine. The people who are most likely to come have been waiting all winter for garage sale season to start. By June, after a couple of months of going to these sales, only the most hard-core shoppers are still driving from neighborhood to neighborhood to garage sales.

WHICH IS THE BEST DAY FOR A GARAGE SALE? Saturday. Again, it has to do with expectations. That's when people expect these sales to happen. Two-day sales—either Friday-Saturday or Saturday-Sunday—often aren't worth your while unless you live on a busy street and you'll attract people who just happen to see your sale while driving by your house. Lots of people work on Fridays, and many people go to church on Sundays, so that leaves Saturday. The other good thing about a one-day sale is shoppers know they can't return the next day for a markdown on items that haven't been sold. Impulse buying is much more likely to occur during a one-day sale.

WHAT IS THE BEST TIME OF MONTH FOR A GARAGE SALE? Soon after the first of the month. A lot of people get paid on the first of every month, or they receive welfare and Social Security checks on those days. Many people make car payments, rent payments or mortgage payments within the first five days of the month. Have your sale before your potential shoppers need to pay these big bills. **Second best?** Soon after the fifteenth of the month. Many of the people who get paid on the first of each month also get paid on the fifteenth. They're feeling a little richer than usual during this time and may be more likely to make a purchase that they don't really need.

WHAT IS THE BEST TIME OF DAY FOR A GARAGE SALE? Between the hours of 7 a.m. and 11 a.m. Seven a.m. has become the most common start time, and shoppers will expect yours to begin by then, too. Assuming the weather is good, garage sales typically stay busy for about four hours. By noon, you'll want to pack up and quit, though you can expect to make occasional sales as late as 4 p.m. or 5 p.m. **The "evil" early birds:** Many people who hold garage sales talk badly about the early birds and urge others to make them wait. If they're willing to pay full price for things you don't want, why not sell to them? Some sellers even make a deal with the early birds: Help me set up, and I'll give you first crack on the items you want to buy. **What you can do:** Price your things the night before, and if you are willing to sell to the early birds, make sure you're set up even before you expect them to arrive. Suspending your setup to make sales with the early birds can put you behind schedule and—if your displays look disorganized and unappealing—cost you sales.

WHEN IS THE BEST TIME TO SELL SOMETHING AT A LIVE AUCTION? Toward the beginning. People tend to bid more at the beginning of an auction. They're excited, their adrenaline is flowing and they have more money. What's more, the largest attendance at an auction is at the beginning. As the auction progresses, more people leave, reducing the number of bidders and the chances for a bidding war. So if you're selling items at a live auction, you want your things sold early on.

WHICH IS THE BEST DAY OF THE WEEK TO SELL HOUSEHOLD GOODS ONLINE? Monday. The most buyer traffic increases on Sunday and peaks on Monday. **Time of day?** The beginning and the end of the workday are the busiest times of day. **Did you know?** The most popular items for sale are sofas, TVs, refrigerators, beds, dressers and exercise equipment.

WHICH IS THE BEST MONTH TO SELL HOUSEHOLD GOODS ONLINE? September or October. Craigslist and eBay report the most activity per user during those months. They theorize that these are the months when college students and recent college graduates are looking to furnish their apartments. The giant online marketplaces say early fall is one of three times when they see the most activity. The other two are January, when people need to buy things, such as exercise equipment, to fulfill their New Year's resolutions, and March, when homeowners do spring cleaning and decide to sell unwanted things. One eBay executive said, "These are the times when people are motivated to organize their lives."

WHICH IS THE BEST DAY OF THE WEEK TO POST ON CRAIGSLIST? It really depends on what you're selling. Job posts tend to get a lot of attention on Mondays and Tuesdays. Personal ads do well on Thursdays, Fridays and Saturdays, and furniture and household ads just about any day, but especially on weekdays. **What you can do:** You may see different results. It's not a bad idea to track your ads to see when they get the most hits.

WHEN IS THE BEST TIME OF DAY TO EXPECT HITS ON CRAIGSLIST FOR BUSINESS-RELATED ITEMS? The afternoon. Work- and business-related items tend to get a lot of hits in the afternoon while people are at work. Post your business-related ads before you go to work in the morning. **Did you know?** In general, Craigslist gets most of its traffic from 7 a.m. to 10 p.m. Eastern Standard Time Mondays through Fridays. Traffic is lightest on the weekends.

WHEN IS THE BEST TIME OF DAY TO EXPECT HITS ON CRAIGSLIST FOR PERSONAL ITEMS? The evening. Leisure and personal items do better in the evenings, after people get home from work and feel more comfortable using their computer for personal reasons. Post your personal ads in the late afternoon, right before most people get home from work so your ads will be new before the flood of traffic starts.

WHEN IS THE BEST TIME OF YEAR TO SELL A VACATION HOME? Spring. Houses tend to look better then because of landscaping and spring cleaning, and there are more buyers in the spring. And those buyers tend to be eager. They've been thinking about this all winter long, and in the spring they very well may have a tax refund check that will help with the down payment. And selling a vacation home in the spring tends to make sense in many different parts of the country. Bankers and hedge-fund managers in the Northeast who receive six- and seven-figure bonus checks in December and January want to buy a second home in the Hamptons or in Cape Cod then so they have time to furnish it to their liking and start using it in the summer. In Arizona, a lot of vacation homes sell in the spring, when the weather is warm and pleasant. By the summer it can be miserably hot, and few people want to buy then. In the Outer Banks of North Carolina, house hunters like to buy in the spring, just in time to start collecting fat checks from northern renters from Memorial Day to Labor Day, a prime rental season.

WHEN IS THE BEST TIME TO SELL STOCKS? When everyone seems to be doing great in the stock market. Don't waste your time trying to predict when the market will reach its peak. Just sell high. When you do, expect some people to look at you like you're crazy for taking some profits. Hold on to your cash from those sales until the stock market is in the toilet and watch those people who looked at you like you were crazy start selling at deflated prices. Then buy what they're selling.

OK, THAT'S FINE, BUT LET'S BE A BIT MORE SPECIFIC. WHICH IS THE BEST MONTH TO SELL STOCKS? May. This is true if you're a day trader or a long-term investor. To understand why May is the best month, you have to understand the significance of November, traditionally the first month of the market's best six-month stretch. If you put $10,000 into the Dow during that six-month stretch—November through April—and switched to bonds during the worst six months every year since 1950, you would have $527,388. The November-to-April stretch is pretty remarkable. Five of those six months have enjoyed an average gain of at least 1.09 percent since 1961. (April happens to be the best-performing month for stocks since 1961, with an average gain of 2.2 percent.) So whether or not you bought a stock in March and saw it do well in April or you bought the summer before and enjoyed watching its value rise from November through April, May is a great month to take some profits. Don't wait too long, though. The market often starts dropping later in May and tanking pretty obviously in June, when others start selling, so don't wait until everyone else is selling. If you do, you very well may leave some money on the table.

WHEN IS THE BEST TIME TO SELL GOLD? When the economy is unstable. During a recession or other periods of economic instability, the dollar drops in value and people look to gold as a good investment. When that happens, the price of gold rises. If you sell then, you're likely to get a good price for it. **Second opinion:** When the Federal Reserve prints more money, as it did in 2011, in response to the financial crises in Greece and Ireland. More money in circulation means each dollar will be worth less, and it will take more dollars to equal an ounce of gold, forcing up the price of gold and increasing the chances you'll get a good price for yours when you sell. **Third opinion:** Some investors believe you should only sell when you really need cash. If you do, then that's the best time. **Did you know?** The value, or buying power, of gold hasn't changed much over the past two hundred years. An ounce of gold cost around $19 an ounce in 1811 and $1,500 an ounce in 2011—which pretty closely reflects the rate of inflation.

WHEN IS THE BEST TIME TO THROW OUT OLD TAX RETURNS? Seven years after you filed them. That's a pretty standard answer, though more conservative tax preparers will tell you ten years or longer. Those who say seven point out that the IRS has three years to audit a tax return if it suspects unintentional errors were made, and six years if it believes someone underreported income by at least 25 percent. *Consumer Reports' Money Adviser* also recommends six years, but many accountants tell you the federal statute that says six years usually doesn't start until the year following the tax year, so play it safe and hang on to your returns for seven years. Along with those returns, keep W-2s and 1099s, statements from brokerages, 401(k)s, IRAs and credit cards, and documents that show charitable contributions that exceed $250. **A second opinion:** Some tax preparers advise their clients to never discard tax returns because the IRS has an unlimited amount of time to audit you if it suspects fraud.

WHEN IS THE BEST TIME TO GET RID OF A CREDIT CARD? When your credit card interest rate is about 15 percent, which is roughly the average credit card interest rate. It makes sense to switch if you've got a lot of debt and you can get a card that offers a zero percent introductory fee. You'll save a lot of money if you can repay the debt before the introductory period ends. But keep in mind that you'll probably have to pay a fee to transfer the balance from one card to another, and you'll need to have a very good credit score—probably around 750—to be offered the best balance-transfer deals.

WHEN IS THE BEST TIME TO SELL COLLECTIBLE SPORTS CARDS? There happens to be plenty of very good times. Here are the best ones:

- Right after a hyped player is drafted. If you think he's overhyped, sell his card. There will be a lot of demand from collectors who think he'll become a Hall of Famer.
- Right after a first-year player receives Rookie of the Year and other awards. Plenty of overachieving rookies experience a sophomore slump and never match their first-year statistics.

- Right after an athlete's team wins a championship. Many collectors focus on players on championship teams regardless of their personal accomplishments.
- Right after an athlete is inducted into a Hall of Fame. Those cards tend to go up in value, especially during a time when the athletes are basking in glory.
- Right after an athlete dies. Again, expect to receive more for those players' cards during a time when the sports world reflects on their greatness.

WHICH IS THE BEST MONTH TO SELL NATIONAL FOOTBALL LEAGUE TICKETS? Early September. As the season begins, fans for nearly every team have some reason to hope that their team can go all the way to the Super Bowl. Tickets, even to see mediocre and bad teams, are easy to sell during the first third of the season. This, of course, changes in December, when at least half the teams have no chance to make the playoffs, and their tickets sell for fractions of what they're worth. **A second opinion:** January. This is true if you're selling playoff tickets. If your team is headed for the playoffs, there is an enormous amount of enthusiasm, and fans will pay much more than face value to see the game live.

WHEN IS THE BEST TIME TO THROW OUT MEAT THAT MIGHT BE GETTING TOO OLD? When it comes to fish, poultry, sausage and ground meat, use it or freeze it within two days after you buy it, or throw it out. Ham lasts in the refrigerator five to seven days after you buy it.

HOW ABOUT DAIRY FOODS? It depends.

- Fresh and soft cheeses, such as cream cheese, are good for two weeks after the sell-by date. Throw away blue cheese if you detect an ammonia smell. Medium and hard cheeses can last for three to six months. Don't worry about a little mold. Cut off any mold you see plus one-eighth inch and you'll be fine.

- If milk is refrigerated at 40 degrees Fahrenheit, it should last for five to seven days past the sell-by date.
- If you buy eggs before the sell-by date, they should last for three to five weeks. Store them in the coldest part of the refrigerator, not on the inside of the door.
- If butter is in the refrigerator, it will last for two weeks to two months after the sell-by date and for as long as one year if you freeze it after you buy it.

CANNED GOODS AND SODA? Try to consume within a year, but if you don't, don't automatically throw them away. High-acid foods, such as tomatoes, grapefruit and pineapple, can last for a year to eighteen months while low-acid foods, such as vegetables and meats, can be fine for two to five years.

DRY GOODS? Sugar, salt and flour can last for several years if they're stored in a cool, dry place. The exception is high-fat flour, such as whole wheat flour, which you should use within two months of buying, though you can probably get a little more time out of it if you seal it well and store it in the refrigerator. **Baking powder and baking soda?** Six months to a year. **Food coloring?** Doesn't expire.

NONPRESCRIPTION DRUGS AND VITAMINS? Two years after the expiration date on the bottle. Drugs and vitamins lose strength as they age. In fact, they lose about 10 percent of their strength by the expiration date. **What you can do:** Store them in a cool, dry place, and they'll last longer, but throw them out if they start to smell bad, crumble, or stick together.

OVER-THE-COUNTER MEDICATION? When the expiration date has come and gone. No expiration date? Toss it one year after you bought it. Old medicine loses its effectiveness, especially if it's kept in a warm, moist bathroom, and in rare cases it can become toxic and cause kidney problems. **What you can do:** Store medicine in a cool, dry place, and when it's time to discard it, don't flush it. Treatment plants find it very difficult to effectively treat medical waste, which eventually can make its way into rivers and streams and poison fish and other marine life. Rather than flushing, crush your pills or soak them in water and put them in the trash. For liquid medicine, call to see if your area has a collection program. Sometimes pharmacists accept outdated medicine.

WHEN IS THE BEST TIME TO REPLACE YOUR TOOTHBRUSH? Every three or four months. Or sooner if your brush's bristles become frayed. That's according to the American Dental Association, which says toothbrushes become less effective when they're worn. The ADA adds that old toothbrushes can also become sponges for germs, and even brand-new toothbrushes sometimes have bacteria on them because toothbrushes are not required to be sold in a sterile package. **What you can do:** Studies show toothbrushes can contain lots of germs even after they're rinsed. If you want to keep your toothbrush as germ-free as possible: (1) Wash your hands before brushing. (2) Rinse your brush for five to ten seconds after brushing. (3) Don't store your brush in a cup with other toothbrushes. (4) Wash your toothbrush in a dishwasher about once a month.

CHAPTER THREE
GETTING THINGS DONE

Buying and selling can take up a lot of our time. Just think about how much time we could save—and how much more efficient our lives would be—if we knew the right times to *do* what we need to get done. Anyone out there want to spend *more* time in lines or on hold or on waiting lists? In this chapter, you'll learn the best time of day to go bowling, run your dishwasher and tweet; the best day of the week to go to the post office and play golf; and the best times to catch someone in a lie, audition for a play and ask someone for a favor.

WHICH IS THE BEST TIME OF DAY TO START A DAILY RITUAL THAT WILL BECOME A HABIT? In the morning. Whether it's exercising, reading the Bible or writing the next great American novel, make sure you do whatever activity you want to become a habit first thing in the morning, before you do anything else, before other things take priority. Behavioral psychologists say this is the best way to start good habits. In the beginning, tell yourself it's something you *must* do. Before long, as you see positive results, it will be something you'll *want* to do before you do anything else.

WHICH IS THE BEST DAY OF THE WEEK TO GO TO THE POST OFFICE? Wednesday. Behavioral studies show many people want to get most of their errands out of the way on Mondays and Tuesdays. Wednesday is the slowest day at most post offices, but they become bustling places on Thursdays and Fridays as businesses and individuals try to get letters and packages mailed before the weekend. **The worst day?** Saturday. Everyone who can't get off work during the week is running errands on Saturday morning. **Did you know?** Some postal employees—especially those in large, busy branch offices or regional hubs—work on Sundays, sorting mail and loading trucks. So even if your post office is closed on Sunday, your letter may still get out that day if you drop it off.

WHICH IS THE BEST DAY OF THE WEEK TO MAIL SOMETHING THAT WILL BE PROMPTLY READ? Wednesday or Thursday. Studies show that mail that arrives on a Saturday is more likely to be read that day, and, in fact, mail that arrives earlier in the week often piles up and isn't read until Saturday, when people have more free time. So if you mail something on a Wednesday or a Thursday, it has a good chance of arriving on a Saturday.

WHEN IS THE BEST TIME OF DAY TO READ A NEWSPAPER ONLINE? The best time, of course, is when big news is breaking, a time when newspaper websites are continuously updating stories and posting photos. And many of the larger papers update stories for their sites a lot. But if it's a slow news day, the late afternoon usually is the best time. Many newspaper reporters work from about 10 a.m. to about 7 p.m., spending a lot of time during the first half of their day gathering information and then writing during the second half. Very often they'll post the first few sentences of their stories online at around 3 p.m. or 4 p.m. and then continue writing their stories for the next day's newspaper until the early evening, when their editors read the stories and then post completed versions online. So late afternoon is usually when you can start to receive the news that will show up in the next day's newspaper. **Did you know?** Many newspapers report that their online readership is highest between 8 a.m. and 9 a.m., when people are getting to work and turning on their computers, and also during the lunch hour, when workers have free time. Some newspapers, especially those with stiff competition, try to give readers something new during the lunch hour so that readers will regularly return to their sites more throughout the day. Why bother? If newspapers can show a high readership during specific times of the day, they can charge more for advertisements then.

WHICH IS THE BEST TIME OF DAY TO POST SOMETHING ON FACEBOOK? Seven a.m., 5 p.m. and 10 p.m. These are the highest, high-traffic times on Facebook, when most people will see what you're posting. These times represent before most people leave for work, before they leave work and before they go to bed.

WHEN IS THE BEST TIME TO CONFRONT SOMEONE WHO "UNFRIENDED" YOU ON FACEBOOK? Never. There are three reasons why you can be unfriended: Someone did it by mistake. Someone had a reason. Someone did it just to get a reaction out of you. In the first scenario, there's no need to say anything. Facebook will send a trillion offers to "refriend" the person you mistakenly unfriended, so your Facebook friend will quickly realize his mistake and refriend you. If the person had a reason, he probably won't want to talk about it, so you'll do a good deed by just letting things be and moving on. And in the third scenario, the person is a jerk and desperately wants you to ask him about the unfriending. Don't do it. Drive him crazy by never asking about it, and consider yourself blessed to have one fewer "friend."

WHEN IS THE BEST TIME OF DAY TO TWEET? Between 4 p.m. and 5 p.m. A number of studies point to this one-hour block of time. One person, a search engine optimization expert, went so far as to say 4:01 p.m. is the best time to tweet for maximum exposure because it's early in that one-hour block of time. **A second opinion:** Others say noon EST. The rationale is that lunch hour on the East Coast coincides with a time when lots of people on the West Coast are arriving at work and firing up their computers, and it also coincides with a time when folks in London and other parts of Europe are leaving work and checking their Twitter accounts one last time before they head home.

WHEN IS THE BEST TIME OF DAY TO EXPECT YOUR TWEETS TO BE RETWEETED? Again, 4 p.m. because a lot of people are tweeting, and plenty of user studies support that time. **Did you know?** The ten most retweeted words (in this order): *you, twitter, please, retweet, post, blog, social, free, media* and *help.* And the ten words that are least likely to be retweeted: *game, going, haha, lol, but, watching, work, home, night* and *bed.*

BEST DAY OF THE WEEK TO TWEET? Thursday. Sixteen and a half percent of all tweets occur on Thursdays, followed by Fridays (16 percent), Wednesdays and Tuesdays (14 percent), Sundays (13 percent), Mondays (12.5 percent) and Saturdays (12 percent). **Did you know?** Only 18 percent of college students use Twitter, according to a recent study of 505 students at the University of Illinois, Chicago. Black students were much more likely to use Twitter, followed by white and Latino students. Why? Previous studies show African Americans are more interested in celebrity and entertainment news, and Twitter has become a big source of that.

BEST DAY TO RETWEET? Friday. Eighteen percent of all retweets occur on Fridays, followed by Thursdays (16 percent), Wednesdays (15 percent), Mondays (14 percent), Tuesdays (13 percent), Saturdays (12.5 percent) and Sundays (11.5 percent).

WHEN IS THE BEST TIME TO USE YOUR CELL PHONE? Weekends and late at night during the week. That's when some wireless companies offer reduced rates or free, unlimited calling. Some also offer these deals during the week but not always when it's most convenient for us.

WHEN IS THE BEST TIME TO DUNK YOUR CELL PHONE IN A POT OF DRY RICE? When your phone gets wet and you want to salvage it. First things first: don't turn your wet phone on to see if it survived its exposure to water. That's a good way to short-circuit it. Assume it won't turn on, and instead remove the battery, dry it off with a cloth or paper towel and put it and the phone in a bowl or pot of dry rice, which does a great job of absorbing moisture. Leave it there for about twenty-four hours. Many phones, including one of mine, have been revived doing this.

SPEAKING OF LOW TECH, WHEN IS THE BEST TIME OF DAY TO KNIT? Late afternoon. This is the time of day when hand-eye coordination is best and when energy and mood levels are up. This also explains why after-school music lessons are such a good idea.

WHEN IS THE BEST TIME TO CATCH SOMEONE IN A LIE? When you know all the signs to look for: (1) Does the person's voice and demeanor change? (2) Does he try to distance himself from the lie by avoiding saying *I* and *me*? (3) Does he have a quick answer for everything that would cause most people to pause before they answer? (4) Is he fidgeting for no reason? (5) Is he saying things like "to be perfectly honest" and "to tell the truth" and "as God is my witness?"—phrases that most truthful people don't use.

WHEN IS THE BEST TIME OF THE DAY TO GO ON A WHALE-WATCHING TRIP? As early as possible. Companies that offer these tours often offer the best deals for trips that start before 9 a.m. **Tip:** Call the company to find out what time of day you are most likely to see whales. The times will vary depending on the time of year, and it may make no sense to go in the early morning if you're unlikely to see anything then.

WHEN IS THE BEST TIME TO SEE STARS IN THE NIGHT SKY? When there's a new moon. A full moon can be stunning, but it pollutes the air with light just as big-city skylines do. With all that light in the sky, seeing stars becomes much more difficult. A new moon lies directly between Earth and the Sun, its dark side facing almost directly toward Earth, making it invisible to the naked eye. With the moon sight unseen, the darkness makes it that much easier to see light from some of the hundreds of millions of stars in our galaxy. **Did you know?** Astronomers say there are somewhere between 200 million and 500 million stars in the Milky Way.

WHICH IS THE BEST DAY OF THE WEEK TO GOLF? Wednesday. Most golf courses report fewer players in the middle of the week, and that translates to less crowded courses. But golf course managers don't like that, so they often offer discounted rates to attract more golfers midweek. However, the discounts often aren't large enough to cause golfers to skip work, so if you're able to hit the links on a Wednesday, you can not only play for less but you also have a greater chance of having the course to yourself.

WHICH IS THE BEST MONTH TO LEARN HOW TO SKI OR SNOWBOARD? January. The end-of-the-year holidays obviously are a very busy time at ski resorts. After the holiday, skiers and snowboarders go home, and resorts are less crowded and often offer great deals on lessons to lure skiers back. It's an opportunity to get individual attention from a pro at a time when the slopes are not crowded, and by January resorts just about everywhere have plenty of snow. **Second opinion:** March. As long as it's not spring break, March is a good time to ski for many of the same reasons: plenty of snow, fewer skiers and good prices. **Tip:** If you were planning a trip to France, you'd probably learn a little French before you went. If you're planning to learn to ski or snowboard, read up on the basics so that when you strap on your skis or board for the first time, you'll know something about what you're supposed to do.

WHEN IS THE BEST TIME TO HAVE A SNACK BEFORE YOU WORK OUT? One hour, and that's assuming you need a snack. You may not need a snack if you've eaten within three hours or if you're not going to be sweating much during your workout. But if you're planning on a long run or a tough weight-lifting session, grab something that's going to give you the extra energy you need to make it through the workout. Some good choices: bananas, apples, yogurt, almonds, walnuts, half a turkey sandwich, red peppers and hummus or soy crisps.

WHEN IS THE BEST TIME OF DAY TO GO BOWLING? In the morning. Many alleys offer specials to get you to bowl when most people don't think of doing it. Some also offer late-night discounts to those who are willing to bowl after 9 p.m. on weekdays. **What you can do:** Make sure you know when your local alley has "league night" and avoid that night. Weekends also tend to be busy at most establishments.

WHICH IS THE BEST TIME OF DAY TO HUNT? An hour or two after sunrise and an hour or two before sunset. That's when deer, rabbits, turkeys and other game birds tend to be the most active, looking for food and water. Although hunters record more kills during these two times of day than any other, they also point out that the most successful hunters dedicate entire days to hunting and have killed deer and other game at any and every time of day, as long as there is enough natural light to see. **Tip:** Some of the best hunters say the very best time of the day to hunt is fifteen minutes before dark. Most other hunters have called it a day by then, and there is less competition for the deer that haven't already found their dinner and resting place.

IS THERE A BEST DAY OF THE MONTH TO HUNT AND FISH? Yes, but it depends on what you're after, and it depends on where you live. *Field and Stream* magazine has a website where you can type in your zip code and find out the best day to fish or hunt for deer or game birds. It's http://www.fieldandstream.com.

WHICH IS THE BEST MONTH TO HUNT DEER? December. Mating season, when deer are most active, is mid-November through mid-January, depending on where you live. Big bucks especially are less careful—and more likely to engage in fights with other bucks—as they pursue females. Mating season coincides with hunting season in most states as wildlife officials count on hunters to thin the herd. **Tips:** Drive as deep into the woods as you can—because deer tend to be less worried about vehicles than they are about hunters on foot—then sit in your car with binoculars. If you discover you need to relocate your deer stand, do it in the late morning and early afternoon, when a lot of deer are resting and won't notice the commotion.

WHEN IS THE BEST TIME TO GET ENGAGED? At least a year after you've known your sweetie. And longer if you're young or have been in a long-distance relationship for part of that year. Some who study marital relationships say many fail because couples don't know each other well enough, and they recommend not even *thinking* about getting engaged until after you've spent six to nine months with your partner. Others say date for five years before you get engaged. Although the answers are all over the board, everyone gives this advice: don't get engaged until you're free of major stress in your life. You want to be able to both make sound decisions and enjoy the experience. And don't get engaged if you feel pressure to do it. **Did you know?** About one out of five couples who got married since 2008 met online.

WHICH IS THE BEST MONTH TO GET ENGAGED? Who the heck knows? But here's a case for December, when the most engagement rings are bought—about 13 percent: 'tis the season when most of us are in the mood to give, and when it comes to engagement rings, we better be in the mood because the average ring costs about $5,500. That makes an engagement ring one of the most expensive gifts a man will ever give his wife, and so it makes sense to do it during the biggest gift-giving month of the year.

WHEN IS THE BEST TIME OF DAY TO BREAK OFF AN ENGAGEMENT? In the evening. This is when blood pressure and heart rate drop, putting less pressure on arterial walls and making it less likely that the person who gets dumped will suffer a heart attack. No joke: heart attacks occur more often within three hours after awakening. One out of three occurs within a six-hour period in the morning. **Did you know?** The American Heart Association takes this so seriously that it has urged businesses to put off announcing layoffs and conducting firings until after 10 a.m. **What you can do:** Before you break off your engagement, give it a lot of thought. While you do it, be gentle and show respect. After you do it, don't give in if your former fiancé/fiancée begs you to reconsider.

WHEN IS THE BEST TIME TO ELOPE? Six p.m. on a Tuesday in the middle of August. Sorry, no, that's not it. I wish it were. That would have been a fun answer. Unfortunately, there isn't a specific answer to this often-asked question. However, couples who have eloped gave revealing answers in a recent survey. For the couples who participated in the survey, the best time to elope is:

- When you want a very, *very* small wedding—just the two of you and someone to officiate.
- When you don't have enough money or don't want to spend many thousands of dollars on a wedding. Brides spend an average of more than $1,000 on their dresses, and the average wedding costs more than $27,000.
- When you don't want the stress and aggravation associated with planning a wedding and wondering if all the pieces will come together on the big day.
- When your family doesn't approve of your intended, or your family and your betrothed's family don't get along.
- When you hate being the center of attention.
- When you've been married once or twice before and don't want yet another wedding.
- When you just can't wait another week—or another day.

Did you know? In two-thirds of all heterosexual relationships, the man says "I love you" first—on average six weeks before the woman. This is according to a study of about two hundred adults by Massachusetts Institute of Technology researchers.

WHICH IS THE BEST MONTH TO ENTER A NURSING HOME? December. No one likes to admit his or her loved one into a nursing home as the holidays approach, and that makes this a time when there are usually plenty of vacancies. After New Year's, nursing home administrators receive a large number of requests for placements and often there aren't enough rooms then, so many nursing homes start compiling waiting lists starting in January. **What you can do:** Finding just the right nursing home for your loved one is one of the most important decisions you'll ever make, so don't rush into it. Here are a few things everyone should do: (1) Do some research. Nursing homes are inspected by state agencies, and those inspection reports are open to the public. Read those, and while you're at it, check out *Consumer Reports' Nursing Home Guide,* which found that nonprofit and independent homes are more likely to provide better care than for-profit homes, that most states are lenient with bad nursing homes and that the nursing home industry has weakened the 1987 nursing home reform law. (2) Visit the nursing homes you're considering several times—at different times of the day and night—and snoop around to see if the rooms and common areas look and smell clean and if staffers are being attentive and kind to the residents. (3) Talk with the staff, from the top administrator to the janitors, and ask lots of questions.

WHEN IS THE BEST TIME OF THE YEAR TO FIND VOLUNTEERS? Not summer. People tend to be less generous with their time during summer. They're busy traveling, shuttling kids to camps and other activities, training new pets and moving. For this reason, many organizations report a shortage of volunteers during the summer and have begun getting out the word that summer volunteers are needed. **Second opinion:** Some companies, struggling during difficult economic times, hire student interns during the summer who gain valuable experience but work for free. **Did you know?** As many as 60 percent of everyone who moves does so during the summer.

WHEN IS THE BEST TIME TO GO TO A MUSICAL OR OTHER THEATRICAL PERFORMANCE? After the second or third show, assuming it's a one- or two-week run. Resist the temptation to go on opening night, when the cast and crew often are working out the bugs and trying to get things just right. By the third or fourth show, lines have been learned, the kinks have been worked out, and cast and crew feel confident that they'll do their jobs well. More important, the actors still have a lot of energy, and it usually shows. If you wait until the last few shows, you run the risk of going when the actors have tired voices or may have lost some of their concentration.

WHEN IS THE BEST TIME TO AUDITION FOR A PLAY? After at least half the other actors have auditioned. More often than not, you won't have a choice. You'll be told to show up at a certain time. But sometimes you'll be told the audition is, say, from 2 p.m. to 6 p.m. on Tuesday or from 1 p.m. to 5 p.m. on Monday, and you can request a time. In those cases, pick late afternoon. There's nothing special about auditioning in the late afternoon, but you'll want to audition after a lot of other actors have auditioned. Why? Very often directors don't know exactly what they're looking for heading into auditions. After at least half the actors have auditioned, directors' visions become clearer and they often begin to change how they instruct the actors—and start telling the actors what they don't want them to do. These things that they don't want the actors to do are often what directors saw actors do during the first half of the auditions. So the actors auditioning later in the process are receiving instructions from the directors that the earlier actors weren't getting—instructions that will help them give the directors what they have decided they want.

WHEN IS THE BEST TIME OF DAY TO SING? It depends, but most singers say late morning to early afternoon, and unscientific surveys bear this out. By this time of day, vocal cords—membranes that snap open and closed while singing and speaking—are warmed up but not tired. The reason it depends is because singers with low voices—altos and basses—tend to take longer to warm up, perhaps because their vocal cords are thicker. Those singers often don't perform up to their ability in the morning. **Tips:** Warm up your vocal cords by humming and singing songs you know. If your throat hurts while singing, stop and lubricate it with some honey and room-temperature water. End your practice session by singing a portion of a difficult song you've mastered.

WHEN IS THE BEST TIME TO RUN YOUR DISHWASHER OR WASHER AND DRYER? During off-peak hours, when fewer customers operate appliances that use the most electricity. Especially during the heat of the summer, when air conditioners are running and brownouts are a concern, some utility companies charge less for electricity during off-peak hours as an incentive to get you to use your big appliances then. Others charge less for electricity during off-peak hours year-round. In New York City, for example, Con Edison electricity is cheaper between 10 p.m. and 10 a.m. on weekdays and on weekends.

CHAPTER FOUR

GETTING AROUND

The Internet gives us the world at our fingertips, and that means we don't have to leave our house to shop, rent movies or go to the post office or to the library. It doesn't mean that we no longer need our cars or public transportation. In fact, it can be argued that never before have we been so dependent on cars, trains and planes for getting us from point A to point B. And in these uncertain economic times, it can also be argued that it's never been so important to know the best times to buy, sell, lease and repair our vehicles and to book airfare. If that sort of information is important to you, read on, and learn the best time of day to get your car repaired, the best month to a lease a car, the best time to sell a used car, the best time of year to buy and sell a yacht and much more.

WHICH IS THE BEST TIME OF THE WEEK TO TAKE YOUR CAR IN FOR A REPAIR? Monday mornings. Many people feel pressure to arrive at work on time on Mondays, so this is the day they're least likely to drop off their cars before work and risk being late. That makes it a bit slow at the repair shop and a good time to drop off your car if you can. **A second opinion:** Some car repair owners say they are slow on Thursdays, making that another good day. The slowness on Monday mornings and Thursdays causes some managers to be willing to charge less to do the work if customers are bold enough to ask for a lower price. **What you can do:** Find out when your local repair shops are slow. These often are days when customers are in the driver's seat and can negotiate discounts for themselves. **Did you know?** Americans spend an average of $5,477 a year on transportation, which includes everything from gasoline and car repairs to bus fare, airfare and insurance.

WHEN IS THE BEST TIME OF DAY TO TAKE YOUR VEHICLE TO A CAR WASH? First thing in the morning. The machinery is cleaner then, and the employees have more energy to dry and detail your vehicle. And some car washes offer better rates before 9 a.m. It's also less crowded then. **The worst time:** Car washes are busiest after 5 p.m. on weekdays—as people drive home from work—and on weekends, especially Saturdays.

WHEN IS THE BEST TIME TO SELL A USED CAR? During—and right after—a recession, when most people feel poor and aren't buying new cars. If they aren't buying new cars, they're holding on to their used cars. With fewer used cars out there for sale, the prices for used cars rise, making it a great time to sell. After you sell your used car, consider buying a new one. Car dealers will offer great deals to buyers then. This tends to also hold true in the years soon after a recession. During the aftermath of a recession, many people are worried about the future and are less likely to buy big-ticket items. In 2011, a year after what was called the worst recession since the Great Depression, car dealers paid an average of $11,660 for used cars or trucks—up almost 30 percent since December 2008. **Did you know?** Since 2007, when the nation's most recent recession began, Americans spent more on used cars, cell-phone services, travel in the United States, lotteries, alcohol, movies, higher education, bicycles, watches and medical care, excluding dental services. And they spent less on new cars, postage, tobacco, boats, jewelry, foreign travel, gambling, museum admissions, clothing repair and alterations and dental care, among other things.

WHICH IS THE BEST TIME OF THE MONTH TO LEASE A CAR? Near the end of the month. This is also true for buying a car, and it's true for the same reason: dealerships have monthly quotas to meet. If you see a car dealership TV commercial that promotes a leasing deal, that often means the dealership is eager to lease cars, and you can try to negotiate an even better deal then. That's right: you can and should negotiate your car lease as if you were buying. If you don't get the deal you want, prepare to walk away. You might just get a call a day or two later from the manager offering you the deal you wanted. **Best time of the week?** Midweek, when business can be slow. **Did you know?** About 20 percent of new car transactions are leases.

SO, WHICH IS THE BEST MONTH TO LEASE A CAR? September. The beginning of the model year, usually September, is best because that's when the banks estimate the residual value, which is the value of the vehicle when the lease ends. Another way of looking at the residual value: it's the value of the vehicle that you won't pay for when the lease ends. You'll want the residual value to be as high as possible. The higher the residual value, the lower the lease price. The highest residual values usually occur in September, at the beginning of the model year. Lease rates typically become less and less attractive the longer you wait after September.

WHEN IS THE BEST TIME TO BUY AN ELECTRIC OR HYBRID CAR? When gas prices are low. When prices are low, fewer people are thinking of trading in their gas-guzzling SUVs for a Toyota Prius or some other fuel-efficient vehicle. And when fewer people are buying electric cars and hybrids, manufacturers and dealers offer the best incentives to buy, and dealers and private buyers are more likely to offer you what your gas guzzler is actually worth. **What you can do:** Unless you want a hybrid car exclusively for altruistic reasons, don't rush into a purchase at what might be the worst possible time. Do the math and figure out how long it will take for a new car to make economic sense, especially if gas prices are high and you can't expect to get much for your trade-in.

WHEN IS THE BEST TIME TO GET A LOAN ON A NEW CAR? There happen to be lots of very good times, and you can save thousands of dollars if you know when to do it. Here are a few:

- During a recession, when fewer people are buying new cars.
- The last few days of the month, when dealerships are trying to meet sales quotas.
- During the end of a model year, which typically is in the fall but can vary, depending on when a manufacturer wants to release a new model.
- When you're looking to buy a car that's out of season, such as a convertible in January.
- When vehicles are falling out of favor with buyers, such as gas guzzlers when gas prices are high and/or rising.

WHICH IS THE BEST MONTH TO SELL A USED MOTORCYCLE? March or April. When the weather becomes warmer, people start thinking about riding motorcycles, and prices for new and used motorcycles remain the same or spike because the demand is high. Dealers as well as private sellers are hoping for top dollar, and they often get it because buyers tend to be eager during the spring.

WHEN IS THE BEST TIME OF THE YEAR TO BUY RECREATIONAL VEHICLES? With gas prices soaring, it's always a good time to buy these gas guzzlers, but the best time is the winter, when it's cold and no one is even thinking about using one, let alone buying one. Because so many people believe that the days of cheap gasoline are over, RVs—even newer ones with very little mileage on them—have become difficult to sell, so consider buying a used one. You might be able to pay as little as a third of what the previous owner paid.

WHICH IS THE BEST TIME OF DAY AND DAY OF THE WEEK TO DRIVE AND LIVE TO TELL ABOUT IT? Between 4 a.m. and 5 a.m. on Tuesday or Wednesday—the hour and days when the fewest people drive and the fewest people are killed in accidents. Nationwide about 100 people die on the road on Tuesdays or Wednesdays, compared with about 145 on Saturdays or Sundays. The fewest deaths by crash occur between 4 a.m. and 5 a.m., when you'll see a mere 9 percent of the traffic that clogs the roads during peak driving hours. The vast majority of fatal accidents occur between dusk and 4 a.m., but it is usually safer to drive during daylight hours, when drivers tend to be less tired and more sober and when more drivers and passengers wear seat belts. Two out of three people who die in traffic accidents at night don't wear a seat belt. Of the people who die in traffic accidents during the day, about four out of ten aren't wearing seat belts. The others suffered such severe injuries that they died despite the fact that they were wearing seat belts. **Did you know?** You're thirty-seven times more likely to die while riding on a motorcycle than in a car. Helmets prevent motorcycle deaths 37 percent of the time and brain injuries 67 percent of the time.

WHICH IS THE BEST AGE TO ALLOW TEENS TO GET A DRIVER'S LICENSE? At least seventeen. That recommendation comes from the Insurance Institute for Highway Safety, and it's based on a review of car crashes involving teenagers. According to two studies, fewer teens die in crashes in New Jersey, the only state that requires children to be at least seventeen before they receive a driver's license. In fact, surveys of parents typically show enthusiasm for raising the driving age, but when state lawmakers propose laws to raise it, that enthusiasm often leads to resistance from some parents who are eager to end their chauffeuring duties. In most states, children ages fourteen to sixteen can get learner's permits, and most states allow sixteen-year-olds to obtain driver's licenses. While New Jersey residents must wait until at least age seventeen to get one, South Dakota residents can get a license at fourteen years and three months old.

WHEN IS THE BEST TIME OF DAY FOR A NOVICE DRIVER TO LEARN TO DRIVE ON THE HIGHWAY? Between 7 p.m. and 9 p.m. At this time, rush-hour traffic has subsided and there is less traffic, but it's still not so late that the driver will be too tired. This time also works because the novice driver will get practice driving during daylight and in the dark. **What you can do:** Follow these steps: Practice driving only if the weather is good. Call first to find out if there are any accidents on the roads where you plan to go. And make sure an experienced driver is with the new driver. Highway driving can be stressful, and the young driver may want to pull over and let someone else drive. **Did you know?** Teenage drivers account for 7 percent of all drivers but are involved in 14 percent of fatal crashes, according to the American Automobile Association. And the number one cause of death among teens is traffic crashes.

WHICH IS THE BEST AGE TO STOP SENIORS FROM DRIVING? When they can't. The percentage of older people who were licensed increased by 73 percent in 1997 and 78 percent in 2008.

The Insurance Institute for Highway Safety doesn't suggest an age, saying it depends on the driver, but one of its studies gives seniors a mixed report card. The good news for seniors is fatal crashes declined 11 percent across the board between 1997 and 2008, but they declined by 21 percent for those ages 70 to 74, by 25 percent for those between 75 and 79 and by 16 percent for drivers 80 and older. The same study shows that crashes-per-mile-traveled increase at age 70 and increase even more after 75.

WHEN IS THE BEST TIME TO GET INTO A CAR WITH AN OLDER DRIVER? When the driver is your grandmother or grandfather. Children were less likely to be hurt in a car crash when their grandparents were driving than when their parents were behind the wheel, according to a study led by researchers at the Children's Hospital of Philadelphia. The researchers examined accident claims in fifteen states and Washington, D.C., from 2003 to 2007 and found that the injury rates were .7 percent for grandparent drivers and 1.05 percent for parent drivers. The results were surprising because plenty of other studies show that older drivers, because of slower reaction times, are more likely to get into accidents. They're also less likely to know how to properly use and install car seats and booster seats. So how can this be? Based on anecdotal evidence, the researchers said grandparents drive differently—that is, more cautiously—when their grandchildren are with them than do the children's parents.

WHEN IS THE BEST TIME TO RAISE YOUR WINDOWS AND TURN ON YOUR AIR CONDITIONER IF YOU'RE TRYING TO GET THE BEST GAS MILEAGE? When you're going 60 miles per hour or faster. In a recent road test, a car traveling 55 miles per hour got 24 miles per gallon with the air conditioner on and the windows up. With the air conditioner off and the windows up, the car got 28 miles per gallon, but when the windows were down, it got 24 miles per gallon—the same as when the air conditioner was on and the windows were up. But aerodynamic drag rises with speed, so if you're going 60 miles per hour or faster, you'll burn less fuel if you leave the air conditioner on and keep the windows up. **Gas-saving tips:** Warm up the engine. Whenever possible, avoid ethanol, which stores less energy than gasoline. Make sure tires have the right amount of air. Reduce idling. **Did you know?** Gas costs 29 cents per gallon more when you drive 65 mph compared with 60, 58 cents per gallon more when you go 70 mph rather than 60 and 87 cents per gallon more when you drive 75 rather than 60.

WHEN IS THE BEST TIME TO CHANGE THE OIL IN YOUR CAR? Every 5,000 to 10,000 miles. What about every 3,000 miles, as Jiffy Lube would have us do? That was truer about fifteen years ago, when oil was made differently and broke down faster. Depending on your vehicle, some manufacturers suggest changing your oil as infrequently as every 10,000 miles. If you take frequent short trips or if you live in very hot or very cold or very hilly parts of the country, then change your oil every 5,000 to 7,500 miles.

WHEN IS THE BEST TIME TO HAVE YOUR TIRES ROTATED? Every 5,000 to 10,000 miles. If you do it less often, your tires will wear unevenly, and you won't get your money's worth from them because they won't last as long. Frequent rotation is like buying insurance for your tires.

WHEN IS THE BEST TIME OF DAY TO CHARGE AN ELECTRIC CAR? At night, if you want to impact air quality the least. Although these vehicles don't produce emissions, the power plants where the electricity is generated do. Researchers found that the least amount of harmful emissions occurred at night, largely because sunlight wasn't around to interact with the particles.

WHEN IS THE BEST TIME OF YEAR TO BUY A YACHT? Winter. This is the best time for two reasons: Dealers want to clear out older boats to make room for new ones. And fewer buyers are thinking about getting a boat. The ones who are thinking about it are experienced buyers, who usually get the best deals. **A second opinion:** Some say the best time is whenever you can get to a boat show. Boat shows occur year-round, and manufacturers there often offer special deals, incentives and rebates on new boats. The shows are also a good place to compare various models and speak with dealers and manufacturers.

BEST TIME TO SELL A YACHT? The beginning of the summer, when demand and prices are as high as they're going to get. **Tip:** Consider hiring a yacht broker. A broker can advise you on the marketplace and on what you can realistically get for your boat. Yacht brokers also know when, where and how to advertise, and they can resolve issues with potential buyers and make sure the title is clear.

WHICH IS THE BEST MONTH TO BUY A NEW KAYAK? July or August. Kayaks take up a lot of space in stores, so managers often discount them then in anticipation of new models arriving the following summer. **Second opinion:** January or February. This is off season, and stores will discount them just to make some sales. Fair warning, though: the selection won't be great. **How about used kayaks and canoes?** November and December are good months to buy used kayaks and canoes from sellers who are trying to raise extra money for Christmas gifts.

CHAPTER FIVE

GETTING PRETTY

Beauty is big business. One year of in-state tuition at a public university—$6,600, by some accounts—is about the same as what a woman spends on average over five years on cosmetics and beauty products. If we did our own manicures and pedicures, each of us could save $9,172 over ten years. About $1.5 *billion* a year is spent on breast augmentation surgery in the United States—about what it costs to launch the space shuttle. Even those who disagree on whether our culture overemphasizes beauty agree that every day a woman leaves her house she enters a beauty pageant—whether she likes it or not. While it's true that a convincing case can be made that beauty has become an unhealthy obsession in America and throughout the world, the fact remains that there is a best time to do things related to our appearance, such as having your hair done, shaving your legs and getting a Botox injection. That's just a small sample of what this chapter covers.

WHEN IS THE BEST DAY OF THE WEEK TO GET YOUR HAIR DONE? Tuesday. It's often the slowest day of the week at hair salons and barbershops so you can get in and out quickly, and barbers and hairstylists don't feel rushed and make fewer mistakes. **The worst day?** Saturday. It's always the busiest day of the week, a day when many stylists say they feel the most pressure and stress. Salons that are open on Sundays are also busy and crowded, as are Mondays, when hair salons say lots of seniors get their hair done as part of their "errand day."

WHEN IS THE BEST TIME TO COLOR YOUR HAIR? When it's slightly dirty. This may seem like the worst time. Doesn't it make sense to color hair that has just been shampooed? Nope. Washing your hair regularly is a good thing to do because a clean scalp is a good thing to have. But when you wash your hair, you weaken your hydrolipid film, a subtle layer of sweat and oil that protects your scalp from bacteria and fungal infections. The film also protects your scalp from hair color products, which can irritate your skin. When it comes to coloring your hair, a freshly washed scalp is a vulnerable scalp. **Tips:** You can color your hair yourself, but it might make sense to have a professional do it the first time to determine the best color for you. And hairstylists suggest touching it up about once a month to keep the color consistent.

WHEN IS THE BEST TIME TO SHAVE YOUR LEGS? Right before your shower ends. That will give the hair plenty of time to soften, and when it softens, it's easier to remove, and you'll get a closer shave. **Tip:** If you're going to the beach and plan to spend time in the water, shave your legs the day before. If you shave that day, the saltwater will find every single nick and scrape, and you may be in a lot of pain.

IS THERE A BEST TIME OF DAY TO SHAVE? Seven a.m. This assumes you tend to cut yourself when you shave. Quick biology lesson: Platelets are the part of your blood that allows it to clot when you cut yourself. They're stickiest and most plentiful this time of day, so if you cut yourself then, you'll probably lose less blood.

WHEN IS THE BEST TIME OF THE YEAR TO SHAVE OFF YOUR BEARD? Spring. This is especially true for men who suffer from allergies. Pollen and other allergens fall into beards and mustaches and get trapped, aggravating allergies and triggering more sneezes and wheezes. Barbers report that spring is a popular time for men—whether or not they suffer from allergies—to shave off their beards, in anticipation of hot weather. **What you can do:** If you love your beard and don't want to part with it, you'll get some allergy relief by washing your face with soap at least twice a day.

WHEN IS THE BEST TIME TO HAVE HAIR REMOVAL TREATMENTS? Late fall or winter. Laser treatments work best when your skin is fair, making it easier for the laser to pick up the pigment, damage follicles and inhibit future hair growth. Many people need about six treatments, so if you start in the late fall or winter, you can finish your treatments, set aside time to recuperate and be ready to show off your smooth skin when summer rolls around. Another answer to this best-time question is when hairs are short. When hairs are short, follicles contain more pigment, making them more susceptible to laser treatments. **What you can do:** To minimize one of the biggest risks—skin discoloration—stay out of the sun after your treatments. That's easier to do in the late fall and winter.

WHEN IS THE BEST TIME FOR A WOMAN TO HAVE A BODY PART WAXED? About a week after your period, right around the time you're ovulating. Women withstand pain better during that time, when their bodies produce the most endorphins, brain chemicals that fight pain and stress. Yes, body waxing—especially Brazilian waxing, which comes in very close proximity to your private parts—can be a very painful experience, but the vast majority of women who do it says the first time is the most painful, and then it gets a little less painful every time afterward. The exception is if you go once a year. The longer the hair, the more it will hurt. **Tip:** If you tend to embarrass easily and you get Brazilian waxes, ask for the same technician every time when you make your appointment.

WHEN IS THE BEST TIME OF DAY TO GET A BOTOX INJECTION? The morning is a good time. You want to have it done several hours before you would lie down and sleep for the night. It's important to be upright for several hours after the injection so that the Botox doesn't drift to a place where it doesn't belong. A shot given near the eyelid to reduce wrinkles and lines, for example, can lead to a droopy eyelid. **Tip:** Botox, which is short for botulinum toxin type A, can take four to seven days to work, so if you're getting it because you want to look good for a special event, have the injection one to two weeks beforehand. Some women get headaches and feel nauseated right after the injection. Botox's positive effects can last for six months or longer.

WHEN IS THE BEST TIME TO GET OTHER COSMETIC PLASTIC SURGERY? When you have the time and support to recover. Give yourself at least a week to recover from the most routine surgeries and a lot longer for serious ones, such as liposuction, breast augmentation and tummy tucks. **What you can do:** Stop smoking. Smoking can slow the healing process and, worse, lead to infections. **The worst time?** Right before a major event, such as a wedding or reunion. Plastic surgeons generally try to dissuade brides from getting breast implants or mothers from getting face-lifts right before the wedding. **Did you know?** The age when most women want plastic surgery is fifty-two, according to a survey of three thousand English women between forty and sixty years old. Twenty percent said they would gladly get a face-lift if they could afford one, and 33 percent said they would rather look twenty years younger than be a millionaire. **And finally:** In the United States, cosmetic surgery occurs more often than anywhere else in Miami, where there are 18 surgeries per 100,000 adults. Nose jobs are the most common form of cosmetic surgery in the Northeast and face-lifts in the western states.

WHEN IS THE BEST TIME OF YEAR TO GET BREAST AUGMENTATION SURGERY? In the fall or winter. Despite this, plastic surgeons typically see an influx of patients wanting new breasts in the late spring, in anticipation of swimsuit weather. Implants can take three to six months to settle, so getting implants in the fall or winter will ensure that the breasts look more natural by the time the summer rolls around. **Did you know?** Breast augmentations are the most common cosmetic surgeries for women, followed by nose jobs and liposuction. For men, it's nose jobs, eyelid work and liposuction, in that order.

WHEN IS THE BEST TIME TO WHITEN YOUR TEETH? As soon as possible after your dental hygienist cleans them. At that point, your teeth are relatively plaque free and cleaner than usual. With all the crud gone, they will more effectively absorb the whitening solution, and you'll see faster results. Just don't overdo it. If you do, you can remove enamel, the hard white surface that protects your teeth. **Best time of day?** The evening, or whenever you feel less rushed and are more likely to do a thorough job. **Money-saving tip:** Over-the-counter teeth whitening kits cost as little as $20, far less than the national average $650-per-visit fee charged by dentists.

WHEN IS THE BEST TIME OF YEAR TO DO A BODY PIERCING? Winter. Fewer people get piercings in the winter, so wait times often are shorter in piercing studios. But more important, having a piercing done in the winter will give your body part plenty of time to heal before it's exposed to the summer sun. Here are some general healing times: earlobes and eyebrows—six to eight weeks; nostrils—three to four months; tongue—four to six weeks; genitals—six weeks to six months; and navel—five months to a year. **What you can do:** Choose a piercing establishment that looks so clean you could eat off the floor. **Did you know?** Winter is also the best time of year to get a tattoo, for the same reasons.

WHEN IS THE BEST TIME OF THE DAY TO GET A FACIAL? The morning. When you get a facial, very often your attendant will apply high-quality skin-care products to your face. You'll want to leave them on your skin for several hours, until you wash your face at bedtime. So when you get a facial, don't go swimming or take a shower until right before bed. Otherwise, you'll cheat yourself of the full effects of the facial.

IF YOU ONLY GET ONE FACIAL A YEAR, WHICH IS THE BEST MONTH TO GET IT? September or October. This allows you to quickly repair skin damage from exposure to the summer sun, which causes, among other things, the outer layers of your skin to harden and pores to begin to close. **What you can do:** Spa managers recommend you receive one facial per month or at least one per season.

WHEN IS THE BEST TIME OF THE DAY TO GET YOUR NAILS DONE? The afternoon. Spas typically use high-quality polishes, which dry slowly. If you get a manicure in the morning you'll have more opportunities during the day to smudge the polish before it dries. Spa managers also recommend you stay out of swimming pools for several hours after a manicure because pool chemicals can wear away at newly applied nail polish.

WHEN IS THE BEST TIME OF THE YEAR TO GET YOUR NAILS DONE? Winter. Healthy nails contain 18 percent water, believe it or not, and the extreme weather we experience during the winter—going from freezing temperatures outdoors to warm, dry air indoors—dries out our nails. And dry nails are more likely to break and split. You need to hydrate your nails, so after you wash your hands, use hand cream and rub it on your fingers and into your cuticles. At night use cuticle oil. If you don't have it, olive oil also works.

WHEN IS THE BEST TIME FOR A BRIDE TO APPLY LIPSTICK? Three to four hours before she walks down the aisle. That may seem too early, but makeup artists recommend doing it then so the bride can focus on her dress and accessories and other things. The color won't wear off if you learn these three tricks: (1) Prime the lips. A primer provides a base for the lipstick to adhere to—allowing color pigments to stay put. (2) Use a lipstick designed for all-day wear. (3) Set lipstick with a colorless gloss that provides a wet mirror shine.

CHAPTER SIX

GETTING RICH

Quick, cover the chapter title with your hand. Now answer this question: What did Jesus talk about more than anything else? (a) prayer, (b) everlasting life, (c) money or (d) hammers and nails. If you guessed "d," well, I'm impressed that you know his earthly occupation. If you guessed "c," you answered this question correctly. If money was a topic that Jesus repeatedly discussed, why not us? This chapter is where you'll pick up tips on the best time to pick up the check and lend money to relatives, the best month to buy stocks and give to charity, the best day of the week to ask for a donation, the best time of the month to lock in on an interest rate, the best time of day to wire money and withdraw money from an ATM. And that's not all.

WHICH IS THE BEST MONTH TO BUY STOCKS? August. Since 1990 August has been the worst-performing month for stocks. If we really are supposed to buy low and sell high, it makes sense to buy in August, when depressed investors often decide—usually against their financial advisers' advice—to do the opposite and sell. Another stinker month is traditionally June, the second-worst-performing month for stocks since 1990.

WHEN IS THE BEST TIME TO BUY AN IMMEDIATE ANNUITY? When you're unable to pay for your expenses with Social Security, pensions and other steady forms of income. This, of course, assumes you also have money to buy an annuity. Let's say you're sixty-five years old and you invest $100,000 in an annuity. It will pay you about $7,600 a year for life. If you live to be ninety, you'll have received $190,000 from your $100,000 investment, regardless of how the stock markets perform. If you die at seventy, you'll only receive $38,000—but you won't really care, right? **Did you know?** Annuity companies don't require physical exams, so they don't know if you're an obese smoker who has had a heart attack and a stroke or if you're thin, in good health and have parents and grandparents who were centenarians. **Keep in mind:** Immediate annuities are reliable sources of income and are attractive to older investors because they're not beholden to stock market fluctuations, but they're not for everyone. They're not for folks who have plenty of money to meet their expenses, even assuming they live well into their nineties.

WHEN IS THE BEST TIME TO BUY INDIVIDUAL LIFE INSURANCE? Before your next birthday. The cost of the policy typically increases a bit with each passing year, so it's cheaper to buy life insurance when you're thirty-six than when you're thirty-seven, and so on.

HOW ABOUT AUTO INSURANCE? At twenty-one. The biggest rate decrease occurs when you turn twenty-one, especially if you've been driving for at least three years. Another, smaller decrease occurs at twenty-five. **Did you know?** In the past, young female drivers paid considerably less for auto insurance than did male drivers, but the difference these days is much smaller. Driver surveys and accident data show that females, especially those who talk on a cell phone or text while driving, are causing accidents at a much higher rate than in the past.

LONG-TERM CARE INSURANCE? The sooner, the better. The younger and healthier you are, the less it costs, and the older you are, the less likely you are to be approved. If you start buying long-term care insurance at fifty, your annual premium might be $1,900 a year, for a total cost of $76,000 by age ninety. If you wait until you're sixty-five and older, you'll pay about $3,250 a year, or $130,000 by ninety. Keep in mind that one year in a nursing home costs about $80,000. **Did you know?** About eight million people have long-term care insurance, and nearly six out of ten of them started buying it between fifty-five and sixty-four, when they were still working but could see retirement—and long-term illness—on the horizon. About two out of ten waited until they were sixty-five and older—the same number that bought it before they turned fifty-five.

WHICH IS THE BEST MONTH TO GIVE TO CHARITY? Charitable organizations will tell you any and every month is best, but December is a great month, especially if you're looking for a great end-of-the-year tax break and you live in a state with NAP credits. Neighborhood Assistance Program organizations help impoverished people by providing food, education, job training, housing assistance, health care and other services. The size of the tax credit you receive depends on where you live. For example, if you live in Missouri and you donate $3,000 to a NAP-eligible organization, you can receive a Missouri NAP tax credit of 50 percent, or $1,500; an IRS tax deduction of about 34 percent, or $1,020; and a Missouri tax rate deduction of $187.50. That means you just donated $3,000 to a charity you love, and your total after-tax cost is $292.50. **Did you know?** Oklahomans give more to charity—$1,587 on average in 2009—than residents of other states.

WHICH IS THE BEST DAY OF THE WEEK TO ASK FOR A DONATION? Sunday. A pair of economists, one from Canada and the other from New Zealand, conducted a study asking for donations at an art gallery. They found that the average donation per visitor was 51 percent higher on Sundays. Others who analyzed the study theorized that people act nicer on Sundays, and churchgoing folks are primed on Sundays with ideas that cause them to do good deeds. The study also found that there were more donors and more donations when the economists posted a sign that said donations would be matched. A third finding: When the economists put $200 in the transparent donation box at the start of the day to encourage more donations, fewer people gave but those who did put money in the box gave more than when the economists put only $50 in the donation box.

WHEN IS THE BEST TIME TO PICK UP THE CHECK? When *you* extended the invitation. If you invited your companion for coffee or lunch or dinner, you pay. If he or she invited you, he or she pays. And that goes for whether you're a man or a woman. The exception is if there's a prior agreement or understanding that the two of you will go Dutch or that you'll take turns paying. In the latter case, pay if it's your turn. **Tip:** Be considerate and reasonable. Don't order four cocktails and a five-course meal if you're not paying. And if you're splitting the check, don't suggest going 50-50 if you ordered an expensive glass of champagne and the lobster and your dinner date had a grilled cheese sandwich and an ice water.

WHEN IS THE BEST TIME OF THE DAY TO WIRE MONEY? Nine a.m., or whenever your bank opens in the morning. Wiring money in the morning gives you the best chance of having the money delivered that day. And if the bank runs into any problems, having started the process in the morning gives the bank more time to solve them and still get the money to its destination that day.

WHEN IS THE BEST TIME OF THE MONTH TO LOCK IN YOUR INTEREST RATE? The first Thursday of the month. The monthly jobs report typically comes out on the first Friday of the month, and depending on what it says, rates can go up or down. Sometimes the market starts getting signals the day before the report comes out. If you're working with a good loan officer, he or she will read the signals and can urge you to either lock in or wait.

IT'S ALMOST NEVER A GOOD IDEA TO BORROW FROM YOUR 401(K), BUT IF YOU FEEL LIKE YOU HAVE TO DO IT, WHEN IS THE BEST TIME? When you urgently need money to repay high-interest debt. This doesn't apply if your retirement plan charges interest of 10 percent or more, but most plans charge about 4.25 percent—much less than what banks and credit cards charge—so it might make sense to use 401(k) money to repay credit card debt. If you borrow $10,000 from your 401(k) for one year at 4.25 percent to repay a credit card with an interest payment of, say, 13.4 percent, you'll save $1,340 in credit card interest fees, and by the time your 401(k) matures, that $10,000 will become $10,425. This almost never makes sense, however, if you have to borrow from your 401(k) because you lost your job. If you're unemployed, how are you going to replenish your 401(k)?

WHEN IS THE BEST TIME TO PAY YOUR CREDIT CARD BILL? Ideally, you'll pay your entire balance every month and never pay interest. Most people don't do that. If you find that impossible to do, the best time to pay is *before the payment date* on your statement, which will save you a little on interest. If you carry a balance, credit card companies charge interest daily until the bill is paid in full, and that interest compounds. On the third day of the billing cycle, for example, you pay interest on the balance as well as on the interest charged on the first and second day of the cycle—a vicious cycle, no? On the other hand, you save a little whenever you make an early payment. And then there's the matter of your credit score. Credit card companies send updates to the consumer reporting agencies about the balances on your credit cards, and they want to know about your debt-to-credit ratios. If you have a card with a $1,000 credit limit, and you have a balance of $800 on it, that's an 80 percent debt-to-credit ratio. The next month, if you make a $400 payment and don't use the card until the next bill arrives, your ratio would dip to about 40 percent, depending on how much interest you paid that month. You want that ratio to be as low as possible, preferably zero percent. Those with very low debt-to-credit ratios on their credit cards typically have very high credit scores—not only because of the debt-to-credit ratio but because they tend to be financially responsible in other areas of their lives as well. **Did you know?** Your FICO credit score ranges from 300 to 850. A score of 800 or higher is considered excellent, 700 to 799 very good, 680 to 699 good, 620 to 679 OK, 580 to 619 poor, 500 to 579 bad and 499 or lower very bad. The median score is 723.

WHEN IS THE BEST TIME TO APPLY FOR A CREDIT CARD FOR THE FIRST TIME? When you need to establish a credit history. There are plenty of good reasons to have a credit history—that is, a *good* credit history. A landlord may want to see your credit history to help him determine if you'll pay your rent on time. An employer may want to see it to gauge your level of responsibility. And most important, a bank will use your credit history to determine what interest rate to offer you if you want to borrow money. So apply for a credit card—preferably not from a department store, which tends to charge higher interest rates—and soon after you receive it, buy something inexpensive. When your statement arrives, pay it off in full as soon as possible. You've just established credit—good credit. Congratulations!

WHEN IS THE BEST TIME TO APPLY FOR A CREDIT CARD IF YOU ALREADY HAVE ONE? There may not be a best time to apply for *another* credit card. First, ask yourself why you need another card. If you don't have a good answer, don't bother. When you apply for a second or third card, a credit check occurs. That check leads to a credit inquiry—sometimes known as a "hard" inquiry—on your credit report, and that can lower your credit score temporarily. These inquiries lower credit scores by about five points, more if you have only a brief credit history. Not only that, but the more credit cards you have, the lower your credit score. The ratings agencies consider you more of a credit risk because you have more opportunity to accumulate debt.

WHICH IS THE BEST TIME TO GET MONEY FROM AN ATM IF YOU LIVE IN A CRIME-RIDDEN NEIGHBORHOOD? Between 5 a.m. and 9 a.m. This is a time when fewer crimes occur and when bad guys—even night owls—are more likely to be asleep. In fact, some criminologists say hourly crime patterns make 5 a.m. the best time to chart the beginning of a new day because the vast majority of drug abusers, bar patrons and partygoers—in some cases, the most likely criminals and crime victims—are in bed or are at least at home. Some workers are waking up, making them less vulnerable to criminals, and the sun will rise before long, making it harder for criminals to conceal their actions. **Did you know?** The average amount someone withdraws from an ATM each month is $411.

WHEN IS THE BEST TIME TO BALANCE YOUR CHECKBOOK? When you receive your bank statement. If you do it when you receive that monthly statement, your checkbook and the statement will be easier to reconcile because you will have written fewer checks by the time it arrives. That equates to fewer addition and subtraction problems to do, making it more likely that you'll actually balance your checkbook. What's more, you are more likely to recall transactions and spot odd activity. **Did you know?** Banks sometimes make mistakes, and most banks give you two months to let them know about any errors you find on your monthly statements. But if you can't balance your checkbook, chances are you—not the bank—made a mistake at some point.

WHEN IS THE BEST TIME TO SAVE YOUR LOOSE CHANGE? When you view it as having little value. If you're not pinching—and counting—pennies, you should save whatever loose change you receive from cashiers or from others. Store it in a big jar or in a sturdy drawer and watch how fast it piles up. At the end of the year—or after a year of saving—count it, put it in coin wrappers and take it to the bank. People who do this report saving $250 to $750 per year. That's money you would have thrown away on gum or a candy bar or something else you didn't really need.

WHEN IS THE BEST TIME TO LEND MONEY TO A RELATIVE OR FRIEND? Rarely. It often leads to strained relationships, battered finances and long-term hard feelings.

BUT LOVE CAN GET IN THE WAY OF A GOOD DECISION, AND YOU WANT TO LEND MONEY TO A LOVED ONE. WHEN IS THE BEST TIME TO DO IT? When the loan is all about business. Hire a company to administer the loan, and make sure the contract stipulates that money from the friend or relative's checking or savings account is automatically deposited into your account on the same day of each month. These companies often charge a onetime fee of about $200, plus a monthly charge of $10 or so. Ask your relative or friend to pay the monthly fee, especially if you're not charging him interest. (And, by the way, you shouldn't charge interest.)

WHEN IS THE BEST TIME TO GET AN ESTATE PLAN? When you turn eighteen. That's right—eighteen. Even if you don't have two nickels to rub together, you should complete a legal power of attorney document, which designates who will make legal and financial decisions for you if you get in a car accident or get sick and become incapacitated. This document is the first of many that will make up your estate plan. Many states have rules that allow parents or spouses to make medical-related decisions for people who can no longer make decisions for themselves, but some don't, so it may make sense to do this. **Money-saving tip:** It can cost $400 or $500 to hire a lawyer to write a power of attorney document. Not getting one can cost a lot more. Those who need to petition the courts for guardianship in order to make legal or medical decisions for a loved one may have to pay $2,500 or more, and that's if it's an uncontested petition. Contested petitions can cost a lot more. **Did you know?** Estate plans can include documents to protect your assets, establish tax plans, set up trusts and spell out marital agreements, among other things.

WHEN IS THE BEST TIME TO WRITE A WILL? When you want complete control over how your money is distributed after you die. Some people assume you should always get a will after you get married, but many states have laws, called default rules, which state that assets automatically go to surviving spouses or to surviving spouses and to their children. If you're fine with your state's default rules, then you might not need a will. But if you want to leave some of your money to your church or to some other charity or to someone other than your spouse and children, then you will need one. Without a will, the courts will decide how your assets will be distributed. Not only that, but your survivors very well may have to pay fees and additional expenses that they won't have to pay if you have a will. **A second opinion:** Some lawyers advise playing it safe and getting a will regardless of the laws in your state. One lawyer joked, "Get a will one year before you need it. In other words, get it now!" **What you can do:** Anyone can write a will. You just have to write it, date it and sign it, and two people who watch you sign it must also sign it. That makes it legal. Not comfortable doing it yourself? A lawyer can tell you about your state's default rules and help you decide whether you need a will. If you do, most lawyers will charge a few hundred bucks to prepare a simple will.

WHEN IS THE BEST TIME TO PUT THE BRAKES ON EXCESSIVE SPENDING HABITS? When you no longer have enough cash to cover *six* months of expenses. Your emergency fund should cover mortgage or rent payments, groceries, utilities, car payments, insurance premiums and credit card payments for six months. If all that comes to $2,000 a month, you should have cash reserves of $12,000, and don't touch it unless you lose your job or have some other financial emergency. **Second opinion:** Three months. This is the case if you know you can easily find another job if you lose yours. But if the opposite is true—if you don't have a high-demand job—consider socking away enough money to cover nine or even twelve months of expenses. **Tip:** It's not a good idea to have too much cash. If your emergency fund will cover more than twelve months of expenses, use it to invest in financial products that will give you a greater return than cash.

WHEN IS THE BEST TIME TO FILE FOR BANKRUPTCY? When you have nothing left to lose. Or, more accurately, when you have nothing left that can be taken. Most attorneys advise their clients to wait to file until they've spent all the money that a bankruptcy trustee is allowed to seize to pay your creditors. So don't file if you're waiting for a tax refund or if you have a plump rainy-day fund or if you can borrow cash value from a life insurance policy, or. . . . Bottom line: Make an inventory of your assets, and then figure out which are protected by your state. For example, many states will let you keep your car, "the tools of your trade," some of the wages you earn, a certain dollar amount of your house and perhaps some cash and equities. Federal law protects your 401(k) account. If you're not sure when to file, contact a local bankruptcy lawyer, who should know the laws of your state. **Another opinion:** Depending on your situation, it may make sense to file for bankruptcy ASAP to delay any garnishments, lawsuits and sheriff auctions against you as well as calls from your creditors or from collection agencies.

WHEN IS THE BEST TIME TO MOVE YOUR MONEY TO AN OUT-OF-STATE BANK ACCOUNT? When creditors are hounding you to repay a debt. That's one tip from self-described credit terrorist Steven Katz, who founded Debtorboards.com. Katz also suggests giving creditors the runaround by using money orders and traveler's checks, which are harder to track; recording your calls with collection agents to try to catch them violating the Fair Debt Collections Practices Act; and suing or countersuing them to drive up their legal costs, perhaps causing them to settle with you or drop you from their list. While these tips are not something you're likely to receive from a lawyer, they tend to strike a chord with a growing number of consumers who lump debt collectors in the same camp with identity thieves and scam artists.

CHAPTER SEVEN

GETTING HEALTHY

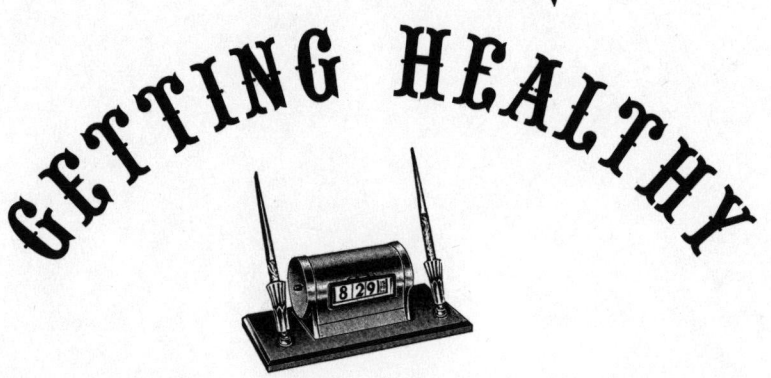

Human bodies have been called the world's most complicated machines. It's not hard to make a case for that. Your body produces forty thousand quarts of urine in a lifetime and two hundred billion new red blood cells a day. Each of our brains generates more electrical impulses in a day than all the world's telephones. Seventy-two different muscles have to interact to allow you to talk. Timing certainly plays a role in the coordination necessary for this amazing stuff to happen. Knowing the time of day or time of month our bodies do certain things helps doctors know how to treat us. And that information can help you, too. After you read this chapter, you'll know the best time of day to exercise, floss, receive anesthesia and sleep; the best day of the week to see a doctor and be admitted to a hospital; the best time of year to lose weight and be checked by a dermatologist; and the best time to take vitamins, calcium and blood pressure medicine.

WHICH IS THE BEST MONTH TO GO TO THE DOCTOR AND EXPECT TO GET IN AND OUT QUICKLY? May. Flu season is over by then, and pleasant weather usually equates to less illness. What's more, in May parents haven't yet started to bring in their children to get physical exams for summer camps and organized sports that start in the fall. **The worst months?** January and February. Doctors offices are crowded with people suffering from the flu and flu-like symptoms then.

WHICH IS THE BEST DAY TO EXPECT SPEEDY SERVICE FROM YOUR DOCTOR? Wednesday or Thursday. On Monday doctors tend to see the most patients, some of whom should have gone to hospital emergency rooms or urgent-care centers during the weekend but didn't because they couldn't afford it or tried to tough it out. Tuesday is still busy due to patients who couldn't get seen on Monday. Doctors' offices typically are less busy by Wednesday and Thursday, making them the easiest days of the week to get an appointment. People who start to get sick on Thursday will want to be seen on Friday, before the weekend starts, so Fridays also tend to be busier than usual. **When isn't this true?** January and February. See above.

WHICH IS THE BEST DAY TO BE ADMITTED TO A HOSPITAL IF YOU DON'T WANT TO STAY LONG? It's not like you usually have a choice, but the answer is Sunday. Those admitted on Sundays stay fewer days than those admitted on any other day, and hospital administrators say that's a good thing because longer hospital stays cost more, use a bed that someone else may need and increase the likelihood for infection. Researchers say this trend, which is several years long, is not because people with less severe problems tend to be admitted on Sundays. Rather, it's more the result of complex hospital procedures. Here's the average hospital stay, based on the day a patient is admitted: Sunday—5.3, Monday—5.6, Tuesday—5.6, Wednesday—5.8, Thursday—6.3, Friday—6.1., Saturday—5.5

WHEN IS THE BEST TIME OF DAY TO RECEIVE ANESTHESIA? Nine a.m. You're four times more likely to have anesthesia-related problems in the afternoon than in the morning, according to an analysis of more than ninety thousand surgeries by researchers at Duke University Medical Center. The researchers found that problems increased from a low of 1 percent at 9 a.m. to 4.2 percent at 4 p.m. The vast majority of the anesthesia-related problems were minor, but the data was clear and convincing that the afternoon presents more risks. Why? The researchers theorized that fatigue and shift changes contributed to some of the problems. Complications also could have something to do with afternoon patients going without food for longer periods, and suffering in different ways from a shortage of fuel and nourishment. The results of this study support plenty of other studies—many unrelated to anesthesia—that recommend patients opt for surgery in the morning, when surgeons and nurses are fresher, are less likely to be distracted and delayed, and are working in well-stocked operating rooms. **Second opinion:** Some anesthesiologists point out a short-term advantage to afternoon anesthesia: patients who are operated on and return home that same day will receive the benefits of that anesthesia for several hours, and it will help them sleep well that night.

WHEN IS THE BEST TIME TO SEE A NUTRITIONIST? Here are four times when it makes the most sense: (1) When you're pregnant or after you've given birth. (2) When you're caring for an aging loved one and need advice to help give them the right foods. (3) When you just want to eat better but don't trust yourself to do the necessary research. (4) When you're an athlete wanting to improve your performance.

WHEN IS THE BEST TIME TO HAVE YOUR HEARING CHECKED? A day or two after you've been born. Many hospitals don't allow newborns to leave until after they've had their hearing tested because about two out of every one thousand newborns suffer from some sort of hearing loss, making it the most common birth defect. The American Academy of Pediatrics recommends that all newborns get tested, and many pediatricians urge three-month-olds to have their hearing checked again. But many children don't have their hearing loss detected until they are about two years old, delaying their language development and restricting their ability to learn.

WHEN IS THE BEST TIME FOR ADULTS TO HAVE THEIR EYES EXAMINED? Every eighteen months to two years after forty-five, the age at which the vast majority of people need glasses of some kind. **What you can do:** If you're wearing drugstore-bought glasses, you're getting regular headaches and your eyes feel tired, see a doctor.

WHEN IS THE BEST TIME TO USE THOSE MACHINES THAT PROMISE TO STIMULATE MUSCLE GROWTH OR HELP YOU LOSE WEIGHT? Never. The machines' electrical impulses do stimulate the growth of muscle fibers, but just barely, and only if you're exercising regularly. So those people you see in the TV ads whose bodies have dramatically changed after using these machines are also working out like fiends. **Did you know?** The Food and Drug Administration has certified electrical muscle stimulation devices for certain types of physical rehabilitation but has cracked down on devices that make unsubstantiated claims.

WHEN IS THE BEST TIME OF YEAR TO LOSE WEIGHT? The winter. Who would have thunk it? Isn't winter the season in which we bulk up and hide our additional poundage under big, thick sweaters and heavy coats? Well, it turns out there's a type of fat that's good, and it's called "brown fat" or "brown adipose tissue." Babies have more of this than do adults, but adults have it, too, and it's good fat because it burns calories instead of storing them. Brown fat goes into overdrive—burning and burning and burning—when we feel cold. A study with mice that were exposed to a 41-degree room for a week lost 14 percent of their weight and 47 percent of their body fat even though they were given a high-calorie diet, including twice as many calories as usual. A study with humans sitting in a room chilled to 61 to 66 degrees also found that their brown fat burned calories at a faster rate than if they were in a warmer room. **Did you know?** Brown fat really is brown. It's filled with mitochondria, cellular power plants in our bodies that break down nutrients and create energy. Mitochondria contain iron and give the tissue a reddish-brown color.

WHEN IS THE BEST TIME OF DAY TO EXERCISE IF YOU'RE TRYING TO LOSE WEIGHT? Probably the morning, as some studies show that working out before breakfast burns more fat. But heart attacks are more likely to occur in the morning, so if you're at risk for heart problems, the afternoon is probably best. When it comes to building strength and endurance, the afternoons probably are best. That's when muscle strength, flexibility and coordination peak. **What you can do:** If you have no major medical problems, work out when you enjoy working out. That's when you're more likely to do it more often. **Did you know?** The five states in which people exercise the most are Minnesota, Colorado, Oregon, Utah and Arizona.

WHEN IS THE BEST TIME TO STRETCH YOUR MUSCLES TO AVOID CRAMPING DURING EXERCISE? There are three opinions: (1) before exercise, to loosen them; (2) after exercise, because it's better to stretch muscles when they're warm; and (3) before and after exercise. Number three is the opinion shared by most trainers and exercise physiologists. However, recent studies on runners and cyclists show that stretching before exercise may steal energy reserves and hamper your workout. **What you can do:** Besides stretching, cut down on cramping by drinking lots of water before and during exercise.

WHICH IS THE BEST TIME OF DAY TO CHECK A RESTING HEART RATE? Before you get out of bed in the morning after a good night's sleep. The average is 60 to 80 beats per minute, but if you're in great shape, it will be as low as 50 to 60. If it's lower than 50 and you're not an athlete, see a doctor. **Tip:** To get an accurate resting heart rate, count how many times your heart beats in one minute while you're still in bed. Any little thing can cause it to rise, and your resting heart rate rises as you age.

WHEN IS THE BEST TIME OF DAY TO BE ASLEEP? From about 9 p.m. to 10 p.m. until about 6 a.m. to 7 a.m. Some people say it doesn't matter when you sleep as long as you get about eight hours a day, but many doctors disagree, pointing out that humans are not nocturnal. Ideally, we are meant to sleep at night and be active during the daylight hours. Here's why: from about 9 p.m. to 11 p.m., detoxification occurs in our lymph glands, making us less susceptible to infections. The detoxification process works best if we're asleep. And then from about 11 p.m. to 1 a.m., a detoxification process occurs in our livers. From 7 a.m. to 9 a.m., our intestines want to absorb nutrients from foods, making that the best time to eat breakfast and a less than ideal time to be asleep. Not sleeping from about 10 p.m. to 7 a.m. also messes with our body clocks, disrupting our metabolism and making it more difficult for us to concentrate during the day.

WHEN IS THE BEST TIME OF DAY TO TAKE YOUR TEMPERATURE? You'll take it when you need to, but keep in mind your body temperature is lowest in the morning and highest in the afternoon and evening. **Did you know?** The standard temperature for healthy people is no longer 98.6 degrees Fahrenheit. It's been lowered to 98.2 degrees, and some people's body temperature never exceeds 98.

WHEN IS THE BEST TIME TO DRINK ALCOHOL IF YOU'RE TRYING TO AVOID A HANGOVER? When you have food in your stomach and when you're well rested and well hydrated. Food absorbs some of the alcohol, and water dulls the effects of the alcohol, which can cause dehydration. That feeling of dehydration leads to a feeling of sickness when the buzz wears off. **Did you know?** Brown University researchers found that people who drank light-colored alcohol—vodka compared with bourbon, for example—suffered less the next day. The researchers pointed out that bourbon contains thirty-seven times more toxic compounds than vodka. They say clearer alcohol typically contains fewer substances.

WHICH IS THE BEST TIME OF THE DAY TO GET A MASSAGE? The morning. Your masseuse is at her best and strongest during the first couple of hours of the day, and most privately admit the morning is when they do their best work of the day. A great massage does a great job of relaxing us, and it's nice at any time of the day, but why not start your day off with one and feel the positive effects of it throughout the day? **Money-saving tip:** If you're a little short on cash, consider calling a massage school, where you might be able to get a free massage from a student. Small shopping center spas often do a great job for half the cost of a country club spa. Regardless of where you go, spa owners recommend you arrive about twenty minutes early to give you time to relax, drink some water and get comfortable with your surroundings.

WHEN IS THE BEST TIME OF THE MONTH TO GET A MASSAGE IF YOU'RE A WOMAN? During your period, if you experience pain. Back massages and full-body massages will relax your muscles, causing your uterine muscles to contract less, which is what causes the pain.

WHEN IS THE BEST TIME OF DAY TO EXPOSE YOURSELF TO THE SUN? The morning. Exposure to sunlight cuts off the production of melatonin, a hormone that makes you sleepy. Morning exposure also causes melatonin production to occur sooner at night, making it easier for us to fall asleep. Not only that, but the sun serves as a natural antidepressant, and it increases the body's production of vitamin D. **Tip:** Doctors say ten minutes of exposure—long enough to walk around the block—is all you need to reap those benefits.

WHEN IS THE BEST TIME OF DAY TO EXPOSE YOURSELF TO THE SUN IN THE HOPES OF GETTING THE MOST VITAMIN D, WHICH HELPS PROMOTE BONE AND MUSCLE STRENGTH? Noon. Not only can you get the most vitamin D at this time, but you also have a small risk of getting cutaneous malignant melanoma, the most serious form of skin cancer, which accounts for about three-quarters of all skin cancer deaths. This is according to a Norwegian study, which says avoiding the sun at noon may be a mistake, and doing so may even promote skin cancer. This and other studies, which also show a link between vitamin D and the reduced risk of cancers, fly in the face of decades of health recommendations that we avoid direct sunlight around the noon hour. The National Cancer Institute's position is that the effect of vitamin D levels on cancer risks remains unclear because research results are inconsistent.

WHEN IS THE BEST TIME TO TAN? Never. At least that's what dermatologists say. All tans, including ones from indoor tanning salons, can cause skin cancer, and sunburns can be particularly dangerous. One sunburn that results in blistering more than doubles the skin cancer risk. **Tip:** If you insist on tanning your skin, choose sunscreen with a sun protection factor (SPF) of 50 or higher. A sunscreen with an SPF of 50 filters about 98 percent of ultraviolet B, the invisible part of the sun that turns our skin brown or red. The sun is so powerful that the remaining 2 percent can easily tan your skin.

WHETHER OR NOT YOU'RE TRYING TO GET A TAN, YOU SHOULD WEAR SUNSCREEN. WHEN IS THE BEST TIME TO THROW OUT AN OLD BOTTLE? Usually when it expires, so check the expiration date. That date is about two years after the sunscreen is actually made, and by then the ingredients have begun to separate, causing the sunscreen to become less effective. **Tip:** Be sure to check the expiration date before you buy sunscreen. Stores sometimes put soon-to-expire sunscreen on sale. Buy it only if you know you'll use it before the expiration date. **Bonus question: When is the best time to apply sunscreen?** About twenty to thirty minutes before you expose yourself to the sun. It takes that long for the sunscreen to properly absorb into the skin. Apply it once every two hours—more often if you're swimming or sweating a lot.

WHICH IS THE BEST TIME OF THE YEAR FOR A DIABETIC TO STAY INDOORS? Summer. Sunburn is bad enough if you're not a diabetic, but diabetics who get burned can see their blood glucose levels rise. And diabetics who are active in the heat need to check their blood sugar levels often because insulin needs can change when heat levels change.

WHEN IS THE BEST TIME TO CHECK YOUR MOLES? About once every six months. Know where your moles are located on your body, and know their color, size and shape. Find someone to check your back and the back of your neck. If the moles are growing or if you see moles that are not tan or brown—say, black or pink—make an appointment to see a dermatologist.

WHICH IS THE BEST TIME OF THE YEAR TO GET CHECKED OUT BY A DERMATOLOGIST? Winter. When your skin is most fair, it is easier for your dermatologist to find moles or blotches that can lead to skin cancer. **Second opinion:** Your birthday. Some dermatologists suggest their patients have their birthday suits checked out on their birthdays. Patients are more likely to actually get checked out annually if they schedule their appointments around a date they'll never forget.

WHICH IS THE BEST TIME OF DAY TO TAKE VITAMIN SUPPLEMENTS AND MEDICINE? Right after a meal. This is often true because while you eat, stomach acid goes to work to absorb and help digest medicine as well as vitamins, which sometimes contain minerals that can upset your stomach. But it's not always best to take vitamins and medicine with food. Always consult your doctor and pharmacist to get the best advice.

WHEN IS THE BEST TIME FOR WOMEN TO TAKE FISH-OIL PILLS? A great time is when they're pregnant. Mothers who took fish-oil supplements while pregnant gave birth to healthier babies, according to a recent study of one thousand pregnant women. The women received 400 milligrams per day starting when they were eighteen weeks to twenty-two weeks pregnant, and the supplements included docosahexaenoic acid (DHA), a key omega-3 fatty acid in fish oil. Babies whose mothers took these supplements were examined at one month old, at three months old and at six months old. At one month and at three months, the babies were 24 percent and 14 percent less likely to have cold symptoms. At six months old, they were as likely to have colds as babies whose mothers took a placebo, but they fought off the colds faster. This is one of dozens of studies that show fish-oil supplements' health benefits to young children. Some of those studies concluded that women should continue to take fish-oil pills if they breast-feed their babies because the children of breast-feeding mothers who take fish-oil pills have sharper visual, mental and motor-skill development. **Did you know?** Doctors say most pregnant women don't consume enough fish, a natural source of omega-3 fatty acids. Doctors advise pregnant women to eat only a couple of portions of fish per week, partly due to a risk that they'll eat shark, swordfish and other fish with high levels of mercury, which may harm their babies. Doctors want pregnant women to eat a wide variety of fish and seafood as long as it's not high in mercury. Seafood that typically contains low levels of mercury is canned light tuna, catfish, salmon and shrimp.

WHEN IS THE BEST TIME OF DAY TO TAKE THYROID MEDICATION? The long-held belief is it should be taken first thing in the morning, and many people take it with eight ounces of water and then wait for at least thirty minutes before they eat breakfast and an hour before drinking coffee. Two relatively small studies—one in 2007 and one in 2010—have shown that bedtime is better. The researchers theorize that the food eaten at breakfast may interfere with absorption of the medicine and that fewer bowel movements in the middle of the night means the medicine spends more time on the intestinal walls. U.S. Food and Drug Administration won't break the tie. It recommends taking thyroid medicine the same time every day, whenever that happens to be. Bottom line: Consult your doctor.

IS THAT ALSO TRUE FOR CALCIUM, ONE OF THE MOST POPULAR SUPPLEMENTS? Yes and no. Take it right after you eat if your supplement contains calcium carbonate, but if your supplement contains calcium citrate, it doesn't really matter. Calcium interferes with iron absorption, so don't take calcium with an iron supplement unless your calcium supplement contains calcium citrate, a mineral used to prevent and treat calcium deficiencies. **Did you know?** Calcium not only helps strengthen bones, but it also helps bone-strengthening drugs work better, and it helps clot blood and regulate your heartbeat.

WHICH IS THE BEST TIME OF YOUR LIFE TO CONSUME THE MOST CALCIUM? Between ages nine and eighteen. Surprised? That's when the National Academy of Sciences says you need 1,300 milligrams a day. The academy recommends 500 milligrams a day for infants and toddlers, 800 milligrams a day for children ages four to eight, 1,000 milligrams a day for those between nineteen and fifty and 1,200 milligrams a day for adults fifty-one and older. **Did you know?** A recent Swedish study of more than sixty-six thousand women concluded that women over fifty really only need 900 milligrams of calcium a day. Taking more is not harmful, but it is unnecessary, according to the study, because it does not lower the risk of bone fractures. **Tip:** Doctors want you to receive the bulk of the calcium you need from food, but if you need to take supplements, don't take more than 500 milligrams at a time. The body can't absorb more than that at once, and the rest will exit your body with urine.

WHICH IS THE BEST TIME OF YOUR LIFE TO TAKE BONE-BUILDING DRUGS? When tests reveal your bones are thinning—there isn't one specific age. Even if you need to take these drugs, don't stop exercising regularly and eating foods that are high in vitamin D and calcium.

WHICH IS THE BEST TIME IN A WOMAN'S LIFE TO TAKE A BONE-DENSITY TEST? Soon after menopause, and every two to three years for women sixty-five or older. Women under sixty-five and men over sixty-five should think about getting the test if they break a bone or are at risk for osteoporosis.

WHEN IS THE BEST TIME TO TAKE A FIBER SUPPLEMENT? Anytime, but make sure you take it at least two hours before or after you take other supplements. Fiber can slow down the absorption of other nutrients.

WHEN IS THE BEST TIME OF DAY TO TAKE BLOOD PRESSURE MEDICINE? There are two: bedtime and first thing in the morning. For most people, take it first thing in the morning, when blood pressure rises, activating stress hormones and leading to heart attacks and strokes, which are more common in the morning. Blood pressure typically drops at night by about 10 percent to 20 percent, giving arteries a break. But it doesn't dip for everyone, and the "nondippers" should take the medicine at night. What's more, those with kidney issues tend to be "nondippers," and high blood pressure can worsen their problems, so they need to be especially vigilant about taking their medicine. **Did you know?** Various studies have concluded that those who take aspirin to combat high blood pressure should also do so at night. Even if their blood pressure drops at night, hormones and other chemicals that cause high blood pressure are more active at night, making that a good time to take some action.

WHEN IS THE BEST TIME TO TAKE ANTIDEPRESSANTS? Whenever you take them, do it at the same time every day. And take them with water, regardless of whether you're eating. It may take as long as three weeks for you to start feeling better. If you don't feel better by then, call your doctor. You may need to try a different drug. If you find one that works, your doctor will probably advise you to take it for at least six months—longer if this is the first time you've taken medicine to treat depression. Be sure to learn about possible side effects and follow your doctor's instructions.

WHEN IS THE BEST TIME TO TAKE SILVER SUPPLEMENTS? Never. Although they are sometimes offered to pregnant women and allergy and arthritis sufferers, they have no known nutritional value, and some studies show they can cause birth defects. Other studies have suggested silver supplements can kill germs, but they're widely believed to be too weak and too toxic to do much good.

WHEN IS THE BEST TIME TO RECEIVE THE MENINGITIS VACCINE? At age eleven or twelve. If you haven't gotten the vaccine by then, do it as soon as possible after that. Meningitis is an inflammation of part of the brain and spinal cord caused by a bacterial or viral infection, and it can be fatal. Doctors recommend children two through ten get the vaccine if their spleen has been damaged or removed. Consult your doctor before you give the vaccine to a child who's ill or who has had a life-threatening allergic reaction to a vaccine.

WHICH IS THE BEST TIME OF DAY TO UNDERGO A COLONOSCOPY? In the morning. Doctors are more likely to find abnormal growths then—which has nothing to do with the colon and more to do with doctor fatigue. A study of 4,665 patients found that doctors working full-day shifts found abnormalities in 26 percent of morning patients and in 21 percent of afternoon patients. Doctors working half-day shifts found about the same percentage whether they worked in the morning or the afternoon.

WHEN IS THE BEST TIME TO GET CHECKED FOR PROSTATE CANCER? Start at forty. That's a good time to get your first prostate exam and blood test. Annual tests should start at fifty. If this sounds familiar, it's because it's basically the same schedule that doctors urge women to follow to check for breast cancer.

WHEN IS THE BEST TIME TO TAKE VIAGRA? Thirty minutes to an hour before sex, though it starts working for some men in as soon as fourteen minutes. The drug can give you an erection for as long as four hours, and it stays in your body for about twelve hours. **Tip:** Avoid high-fat foods two hours before taking it. That can slow your body's ability to absorb the drug, also slowing down its ability to work faster.

WHEN IS THE BEST TIME TO SEEK MALE INFERTILITY TREATMENT? After you've tried to conceive for at least a year. After that amount of time, doctors say it's reasonable to start gathering information about infertility treatment. Sometimes the treatment is as simple as stopping smoking, wearing loose-fitting underwear, changing your diet or taking supplements or medicine. Other times it involves working with sperm, and that may include surgery. **Did you know?** When a couple can't get pregnant, male infertility is the cause about 40 percent of the time. Treatment helps about half of those men become fathers.

HOW ABOUT FOR FEMALES? After a year of trying to pregnant, unless the woman is thirty-five or older. If you're thirty-five or older, see your doctor after six months of trying. A woman's chances of getting pregnant decrease rapidly after thirty. Health problems, such as painful or irregular periods or previous miscarriages, can make it more difficult to get pregnant. **What you can do:** Regardless of how long you've been trying to get pregnant, it's always a good idea to talk with your doctor, who can answer your questions and give you tips to help you conceive.

WHEN IS IT BEST TO USE A COTTON SWAB TO CLEAN THE WAX OUT OF YOUR EARS? Never. Using a Q-tip or cotton swab can damage the ear canal lining, or you can push the wax deeper into the ear canal, and that can cause hearing loss and other issues, such as infections. Doctors say you don't need cotton swabs at all because the wax has a way of eventually working its way out of your ears on its own. If you don't want to wait for that to happen, you can use eardrops if you are not susceptible to ear infections. **Tip:** You can make your own safe and inexpensive eardrops by mixing a teaspoon of baking soda with two ounces of warm water.

WHEN IS THE BEST TIME OF DAY TO REMOVE EXTENDED-WEAR CONTACT LENSES? At night, before you go to sleep. If you wear extended-wear lenses, you're ten to fifteen times more likely to develop corneal ulcers than if you wear daily-wear contacts. **What you can do:** Make sure you have clean hands before you remove your lenses. Wash your hands with soap that doesn't have a lot of perfume or moisturizer, such as aloe, in it.

WHEN IS THE BEST TIME TO START USING DECONGESTANTS? After you've tried nondrug treatments, such as inhaling steam and drinking fluids. Try nasal products first because they tend to work better and cause fewer side effects. **Caution:** Nasal drops and sprays can cause "rebound congestion," or renewed stuffiness that can be worse than the original congestion. If the congestion lingers for more than three days, switch to oral decongestants.

IF YOU'RE TRAVELING ABROAD, WHEN IS THE BEST TIME TO GET A FLU SHOT? A couple of weeks before you leave. The flu season in the United States starts in late October and ends in late March, but international travelers can get the flu just about any month of the year. Flu shots can take about two weeks to work, so keep that in mind if you plan to get one before you leave the country. **Bonus question: What if you're staying in the United States?** October is considered the best month, but anytime between September and February makes sense. The vaccine is supposed to last 180 days—the length of the flu season—but very often it lasts only about 90, so you'll still get plenty of protection out of it in, say, January, if you haven't gotten it by then.

WHEN IS THE BEST TIME TO SEE YOUR DOCTOR IF YOU CAN'T GET RID OF COLD SORES, ALSO CALLED FEVER BLISTERS? After fourteen days. Cold sores—lesions caused by a herpes virus to which most adults have been exposed—can't be cured or prevented, but you can limit them. The best treatment seems to be prescription acyclovir pills, not the cream. See a doctor if you have several outbreaks a year. **Did you know?** A team of Harvard and Duke researchers discovered that the virus that causes cold sores hides in nerve cells, and they hope that information will lead to a cure. **Finally:** Cold sores and canker sores are not the same thing. Canker sores, also called mouth ulcers, are white or yellow and are always found inside the mouth while cold sores often are on the lips and mouth.

WHEN IS THE SOONEST YOU SHOULD TRY TO CONCEIVE AFTER GIVING BIRTH? Wait at least a month. Becoming pregnant immediately after giving birth isn't known to cause problems to mother or child, but waiting a month or longer gives you time for your menstrual period to become regular, and that makes it easier to figure out your due date when you get pregnant again. It's also not a bad idea to allow your body at least a month to heal before getting pregnant again.

WHEN IS THE BEST TIME TO RECEIVE A PELVIC EXAM OR SEE YOUR OBSTETRICIAN AND/OR GYNE-COLOGIST? Right after your period ends. Your cervix is softer so the exam will be more comfortable, and it's also more open so your doctor can get a more accurate sample.

WHEN IS THE BEST TIME FOR GIRLS TO GET THE HPV (HUMAN PAPILLOMAVIRUS) VACCINE? Age eleven or twelve. The Centers for Disease Control and Prevention recommends this time—before girls are exposed to sexual contact—and it encourages women as old as twenty-six to receive the vaccine. Human papillomavirus is the most common sexually transmitted disease in the United States, and the vaccine can protect girls and women from the virus and prevent most cases of cervical cancer as well as vaginal and vulvar cancers. Girls as young as nine can get the vaccine, which comes in three doses. Although boys as young as nine may also get the vaccine to prevent genital warts, the CDC's recommendation is only for girls. The shot hurts and could lead to fever and headaches, but it is considered very safe. At least twenty states have passed a law to require girls to receive the vaccine, but parents can opt out. Some parents say vaccinating sends a signal to girls that it's OK to have sex and that they are safe from all sexually transmitted diseases. **What you can do:** If you decide your child should receive the vaccine, choose Gardasil if you have a choice. There are actually two approved vaccines, Cervarix and Gardasil, and both are considered safe and effective against HPV types 16 and 18, which cause most cervical cancers. But only Gardasil also protects against HPV types 6 and 11, which cause most genital warts, has been licensed for use by males and has been shown to protect against cancers of the vulva, vagina and anus.

WHEN IS THE BEST TIME TO TAKE A GIRL TO HER FIRST APPOINTMENT WITH A GYNECOLOGIST? Age fourteen to sixteen. The first visit includes a cervical exam only if the girl is experiencing an unusual amount of pain or is sexually active. Otherwise, it usually consists only of a consultation, so that the doctor can get to know the girl, educate her about menstruation and answer questions she may have. **What you can do:** A parent—mother, ideally—should attend the appointment with the child, but be willing to leave the room if the child wants to speak confidentially to the doctor. **Bonus question: How about a woman's first cervical exam?** Twenty-one, according to the American College of Obstetricians and Gynecologists.

WHEN IS THE BEST TIME TO DO A BREAST EXAM ON YOURSELF? When your breasts are not tender and swollen. Even doctors differ on the timing of this, but the American Cancer Society says if you do it when your breasts are not swollen, you're more likely to find a lump or some other abnormality. And if you do it when your breasts are not tender, you're more likely to be more thorough because it won't be painful. **What you can do:** All adult women should examine their breasts monthly. Women under forty should have a professional examine their breasts once every three years, and women older than that should have their breasts examined by a health-care professional once a year.

HOW ABOUT A MAMMOGRAM? Same as when you do your own exam. Not only will it hurt less when your breasts are not tender or swollen, but the technician will get a better, clearer image.

WHEN IS THE BEST TIME TO GET A ROOT CANAL OR UNDERGO SOME OTHER SORT OF PAINFUL PROCEDURE? When you're ovulating. During this time, women's bodies produce the most endorphins, brain chemicals that fight pain and stress. **The worst time?** Right before your period.

WHEN IS THE BEST TIME TO GET A HYSTEROSCOPY? During the first week after your period. A hysteroscopy provides a way for your doctor to examine your uterus by using an instrument like a telescope that helps diagnose uterine problems. During the first week after your period, your doctor has the best opportunity to view the inside of the uterus.

WHEN IS THE BEST TIME TO PERFORM A CIRCUMCISION? When the child is a newborn. During this time, circumcision is less likely to lead to infections, and it's more convenient and less expensive because the child is already at the hospital. The child won't remember the pain associated with it, and he has elevated levels of normal stress-resistance hormones because of the trauma of childbirth. What's more, babies heal quickly and are resilient. Circumcisions for older children and adults cost more, hurt more and heal slower. **Did you know?** The American Academy of Pediatrics and the American Medical Association acknowledge the benefits of circumcisions but they don't encourage or recommend them. Rather, they say it's a decision parents need to make.

WHEN IS THE BEST TIME TO STRENGTHEN YOUR TEETH? While you eat. During this time, more saliva is released, helping to wash away food particles and plaque and lessen the effect of acids that cause tooth decay. **Tip:** Dentists recommend brushing for at least three minutes, making sure to clean the front and back of each tooth.

DENTISTS SAY NOTHING TAKES THE PLACE OF FLOSSING, SO WHICH IS THE BEST TIME OF DAY TO DO IT? Right before bed. Many dentists advise their patients to floss whenever they have the time to do it right, but there is some evidence that bedtime is the best time. You want the inside of your mouth to be its cleanest while you sleep because at night the flow of saliva decreases. That's significant because saliva helps combat the effects of bacteria in our mouths. What's more, if you floss at night you're less likely to rush than if you do it in the morning when you're getting ready for work. **Bonus question: How many times a day should you floss?** Once is enough if you do it right, gently touching your gums with the floss between each tooth. Twice is great. **What you can do:** Whenever you decide to floss, rinse your mouth with water or mouthwash afterward so you can spit out the food particles you dislodged while you flossed. **Did you know?** Residents of Connecticut, Massachusetts, Rhode Island, Delaware and New Hampshire are more likely to see their dentists on a regular basis.

WHEN IS THE BEST TIME FOR WOMEN TO GO TO THE DENTIST? After menopause. Of course women should see their dentist regularly—once or twice a year—but women don't have enough estrogen after menopause, and without this hormone, they are more susceptible to inflammation—and periodontal disease. Women of this age need to go to the dentist more often to remove the plaque that can cause gum disease and weaken jaw bones. An insufficient amount of estrogen also makes women more susceptible to osteoporosis.

WHEN IS THE BEST TIME FOR AN ADULT WHO NEEDS BRACES TO GET THEM? The sooner, the better. Adults obviously can—and do—get braces, but adult teeth move more slowly and usually try to shift back to their original position. The longer teeth are misaligned, the longer it will take to get them back where they need to be, so adults should get braces or aligners—a good option when minor changes are needed—as soon as they realize they need work done. **Did you know?** One in five orthodontic patients is an adult.

WHEN IS THE BEST TIME TO EAT SALMON, STRAWBERRIES, WHOLE-GRAIN BREAD AND PISTACHIOS? When you want healthier gums. Yep, each of these foods—and green tea—contains vitamins and antioxidants that help your gums. Salmon has lots of omega-3 fatty acids, which reduce inflammation, and consuming omega-3 fatty acids has been linked to a reduced risk of gingivitis. Vitamin C–rich strawberries produce collagen, which helps keep gum tissue healthy. One large study found that people who eat three servings a day of whole-grain bread, which contains iron and B vitamins, reduced the chances of gum disease by 23 percent. Pistachios contain a lot of CoQ10, an antioxidant that fights gum inflammation. And green tea—hot or cold—kills the bacteria that cause gingivitis.

WHEN IS THE BEST TIME TO GET A SECOND OPINION WHEN YOUR DOCTOR OR DENTIST RECOMMENDS MAJOR DENTAL WORK? This will be hard one to swallow—get it?—for many people, but the answer is every time. We become attached to our doctors and dentists and don't want to hurt their feelings by questioning their advice. But a second opinion likely will reassure you that you need the work done, and if the second opinion comes from a specialist, he or she may give you information that your doctor or dentist didn't have the knowledge to provide.

WHEN IS THE BEST TIME TO APPLY FOR MEDICARE? Three months before your sixty-fifth birthday. Applying online is easy. Go to http://www.ssa.gov/medicareonly/.

CHAPTER EIGHT

GETTING THE JOB DONE

I learned that we can do anything, but we can't do everything—at least not at the same time. So think of your priorities not in terms of what activities you do, but when you do them. Timing is everything.

—Dan Millman, American self-help author and philosopher

Millman's words ring especially true in the workplace, where good time management eludes so many people. Knowing when to do things—and not do things—can mean the difference between getting a job, getting promoted and getting good attendance at a meeting. Read on if you want to know the best time of day to interview for a job, start your work and read reports, the best month to buy office furniture and hold an out-of-town meeting and the best day of the week to call your financial adviser and your lawyer.

IF YOU HAVE A CHOICE, WHEN IS THE BEST TIME OF DAY TO INTERVIEW FOR A JOB? Ten a.m., 11 a.m., or 3 p.m. If you interview at 9 a.m., the interviewer may have just arrived at work, may feel rushed and unprepared, and may find it difficult to focus on you. Right after lunch, people often feel sleepy and find it hard to focus. At 4 p.m. and later, interviewers often are tired and thinking more about going home than about anything else. **Another view:** Pick a time based on what's best for you. If you're a morning person and are especially sharp then, ask for the earliest time you can get. Whatever time of day you think you're at your best is a good time because you'll be more confident, and your confidence may help you land the job.

WHEN IS THE BEST ORDER IN WHICH TO INTERVIEW FOR A JOB—FIRST OR LAST? The conventional wisdom is first is worst because the company will forget about you and your attributes by the time it ends up making a hiring decision. There's even a study that shows about 55 percent of the people who interview last get the job while only 17 percent of those who interview first do. Some hiring managers admit it's easier to remember the candidates who interview last. But most say those who think it's best to go last aren't giving the interviewers enough credit. They say hiring managers can keep track of the best candidates and usually make the right choices, whether the job seekers interview first, last or in the middle of the pack.

WHICH IS THE BEST DAY OF THE WORKWEEK TO GET SOMETHING ACCOMPLISHED? Tuesday. It's the most productive day of the workweek by far, according to a survey of 150 senior executives at the nation's largest firms. About 57 percent of the executives chose Tuesday, followed by Monday (12 percent), Wednesday and Thursday (11 percent each) and Friday (3 percent). If you're doing the math, that adds up to only 94 percent. Six percent of the executives said they had no idea which day was most productive. Those who chose Tuesday said many workers get their marching orders for the week on Monday, and they view Tuesday as a day to focus their efforts and gather momentum for the rest of the week. And they're not yet distracted by upcoming weekend plans.

WHICH IS THE BEST DAY OF THE WEEK TO ASK A CO-WORKER FOR A FAVOR? Thursday or Friday. Plenty of workplace studies show that we become more agreeable toward the end of the workweek. There is a strong desire to avoid conflict as the weekend approaches, and people just want to make it through another week and get to the weekend. Thursday may be the better of the two days. On Fridays, workers are thinking more about their weekend plans and may be less inclined to commit to something that will require them to give their time or money.

WHEN IS THE BEST TIME OF DAY TO READ REPORTS? Early afternoon. This is a time when our body temperature is low and we fight sleep, but it's also a time when optometrists say our vision is sharpest. If you can see the words better then and reading is easier, you're more likely to concentrate on what you're reading and understand it better.

WHICH IS THE BEST MONTH TO ASK FOR A PROMOTION? January. This is the case if your company's fiscal year mirrors the calendar year. These companies start working on next year's budget in the fall, usually finishing up in November. There is often still money to spend late in the year—and in fact, more hiring occurs in December than most people realize—but many companies look to save money then in order to increase profit margins, especially when those profit margins are tied to managers' bonuses. Wait until early in the year to ask for a promotion, when companies, flush with the new fiscal year, are in spending mode and few are thinking about how your promotion—and the pay raise that goes with it—will impact the bottom line. **Did you know?** Sixteen percent of all promotions since 2000 occurred in January, the largest percentage by month. **Second opinion:** July. Ask then when most businesses are slow. If you get promoted, you have a couple of months to get up to speed before things pick up in the fall. July is also the beginning of the fiscal year for some companies, so those firms are in spending mode then. **Tip:** To give yourself the best chance to get a promotion, plan for it year-round by updating your supervisor on all the good things you're doing and making it clear to him or her that you want to advance in the company. Rather than waiting until the day of your annual job review to toot your own horn, give your supervisor a monthly or quarterly report with your accomplishments. Chances are he or she will use those reports to help him or her write your performance evaluation. A lazy supervisor will cut and paste your comments right into your job review, in effect letting you write your own review. Wouldn't you give yourself a promotion? **Did you know?** In a recent survey, 83 percent of human resources professionals say they form opinions about employees based on how their workspace looks. As you might expect, clean desks score brownie points with the HR types.

WHEN IS THE BEST TIME OF DAY TO START WORK AND EXPECT LESS FATIGUE IN THE WORKPLACE?

Nine a.m. People who start work at 9 a.m. tend to get more sleep per day—about eight hours—than people who start work at different times, so they are less likely to experience on-the-job fatigue. Those whose shifts start at 11 p.m. are the most likely to experience fatigue at work because they sleep an average of only four and a half hours per day, according to a study by University of Washington, Spokane, researchers. Many of those who start work at 11 p.m. don't sleep before work while those who start at midnight often do sleep an hour or two. The researchers attribute that to our body's circadian rhythm, a daily cycle of activity found in people and other animals. This cycle exists regardless of what time of day we work, and many other studies conclude that people who work late at night or in the early morning are more vulnerable to sickness and disease because they sleep and exercise less and don't eat as well as others.

WHEN IS THE BEST TIME TO FIND A HEADHUNTER TO HELP YOU FIND A JOB? When you make at least $100,000 a year and when you don't need another job. Let's start with the first part of the answer. If you don't make at least $100,000 a year, most headhunters won't be interested in helping you because they get paid based on your starting salary, and they don't make much money if you're likely to get hired for only a five-figure job. If you make more than $100,000 a year at your current job and it's likely you'll leave the company at some point, start talking with headhunters at prestigious firms so that when the time comes for you to begin your job search, you'll have built a relationship with two or three of them and you can make a good decision about which one you want to hire. **Tip:** Headhunters often hear about executive job seekers from others. If a headhunter "cold calls" you, be courteous and professional or you can be blacklisted, making it more difficult to find a good headhunter when you need one.

WHEN IS THE BEST TIME TO ANNOUNCE YOUR RETIREMENT? At least one month before you want to leave. Many pension or 401(k) plans require at least a month to get the documents ready for your departure. If you wait until those documents are ready, there won't be a large gap, if any, between your final regular paycheck and your first pension check. If you're a valuable employee who gets along well with all the right people and you want to stay with the company as a consultant after you retire, give as much as six months' notice. Your supervisor will appreciate that extra time to fill your job and to figure out how to best use you as a consultant. But don't announce your retirement too early—say, a year or more. The employee who does risks being removed from important work or even demoted by supervisors who assume the person has checked out mentally and no longer cares about the company. **Tip:** Whenever you make the announcement, try to do it during a period when you are working on a high-profile project or are otherwise very productive. Many times an employer will try to incentivize a particularly valuable employee to delay retirement plans or will offer a lucrative consulting gig without the person having to ask for it.

WHICH IS THE BEST DAY TO EXPECT GOOD ATTENDANCE AT A MEETING? Mondays. Many employees expect to sit in meetings on Monday, in some cases to get their marching orders for the rest of the week. Tuesdays or Wednesdays are the most productive days of the workweek, so many managers don't want their employees stuck in meetings on those days. **Did you know?** Friday, which is largely considered the least productive day of the week, is the day workers are most likely to call in sick. But according to a recent survey, the first Monday in February is the most likely day of the entire year that workers will call in sick. Healthy workers who admit to doing this sometimes blame cold, nasty weather for not wanting to leave the house. And those who work on Martin Luther King Jr. Day and Presidents' Day say they need a day off between New Year's and Easter.

WHEN IS THE BEST TIME OF DAY TO HOLD A MEETING TO EXPECT THE BEST ATTENDANCE? About thirty minutes after everyone is expected at work. This time allows even stragglers to attend the meeting, and because it's so early in the workday, other workers won't have had much time to get distracted with other work-related issues that might keep them from attending the meeting. **What you can do:** If you hold a morning meeting, make sure employees know about it the day before so they'll come prepared. The early notification also means they'll be more likely to be on time. **Did you know?** A growing number of companies are holding "Swiss-time meetings," scheduling them at times such as 9:32 a.m. or 1:13 p.m.

Doing this makes the meeting time stand out more in the employees' minds, and the companies say more workers show up on time for meetings scheduled at odd times.

WHEN IS THE BEST TIME TO HIRE TALENTED WORKERS? When your company is laying off people. Yeah, that's right. That's the best time to hire the best job seekers. People who get laid off often have one or more of these things in common: they're unproductive or underproductive. They're looking to take early retirement and they've mentally checked out. Or they're doing tasks that others can easily do, making them expendable. As you lay off these folks, make an investment in the company by replacing those employees with workers who directly generate revenue, step into hard-to-find jobs or move the company down a new, lucrative path.

WHEN IS THE BEST DAY OF THE WEEK TO CALL YOUR FINANCIAL ADVISER? Friday. It's often the slowest day of the week, when advisers schedule fewer meetings, giving you a better chance to get through to yours. Advisers also say they're usually in good moods on Friday, a day when they're looking forward to the weekend. **The worst day?** Monday. This is usually the most hectic day of the workweek for advisers, who are scrambling to help clients who called or e-mailed with requests over the weekend as well as trying to finish any scheduled work from the prior week and plan the new week.

WHEN IS THE BEST TIME TO CALL A CRIMINAL DEFENSE LAWYER? Before you answer questions from the police. You only need to tell police your name. After that, criminal defense lawyers urge you to tell the police, "I'd like to cooperate with your investigation, but first I need to talk with my lawyer." Continue saying this, they say, even if the police say something like, "Well, I only have a few questions for you." Make it clear that you want to cooperate, but don't relent: tell them you need to speak with your lawyer. The lawyers say their job, among other things, is to protect your rights, including your right to remain silent.

WHEN IS THE BEST TIME OF DAY TO CALL YOUR LAWYER AND EXPECT A QUICK CALL BACK? The afternoon. Lawyers are often in court in the morning, or they're in meetings with clients or with their partners. Many reserve the afternoon for catching up on work or returning clients' phone calls. And many lawyers try to return phone calls the day they receive them, so if you call in the afternoon don't be surprised to receive a call back that day, even if it's as late as 8 p.m. or 9 p.m. This has an added benefit for lawyers, many of whom say they get brownie points from their clients when they return phone calls at a time they are expected to be at home with their families. **Second opinion:** Nine a.m. Some lawyers return phone calls in the order they're received, so even if your lawyer is in court or in meetings in the morning, you may receive a call back in the early afternoon if you call as soon as his or her office starts receiving phone calls.

WHICH IS THE BEST MONTH TO BUY OFFICE FURNITURE AND EQUIPMENT? April or May. Office supply stores know that a lot of home-based businesses start up when they have the money to do so, and that's often right after their owners received their tax refund checks. You can save at least 25 percent and often more on desks, filing cabinets and leather desk chairs in the spring. **Second opinion:** January. The start of a new year is when many fledgling entrepreneurs decide to start their businesses, and some office supply stores attribute increased sales to January start-ups.

WHEN IS THE BEST TIME TO HIRE COMPUTER GEEKS NOT ASSOCIATED WITH YOUR COMPUTER'S MANUFACTURER? Here are three very good times: (1) When the source of the problem isn't obvious. Most manufacturers' techies examine only preinstalled hardware and software covered by the warranty while independents usually go beyond that. (2) When a virus or spyware is wreaking havoc. In a recent survey, independent geeks found the culprits 25 percent of the time, as opposed to only 8 percent for manufacturers' tech support. (3) When you want easy phone support. In that survey, only 12 percent of users reported problems with the independents versus 58 percent who spoke with the manufacturers' staff.

WHICH ARE THE BEST DAYS OF THE WEEK TO SCHEDULE AN OUT-OF-TOWN CONFERENCE, TRAINING PROGRAM OR BOARD MEETING? The weekend. Hotels, especially in big cities, struggle to book rooms on weekends. The highest vacancies typically occur on Sundays and Mondays, so if your employees fly in on a Sunday, you can get the best room rates. Expect to save 20 percent to 25 percent then. **Did you know?** Conference centers and hotels will reduce rates for groups that plan to do more than meet. Groups that commit to buying meals at the hotel or using the spa, for example, get lower rates than those that plan to use a meeting room and then leave the hotel or conference center to eat.

WHICH IS THE BEST MONTH TO HOLD AN OUT-OF-TOWN MEETING? July or August. Those are the cheapest months to do it. Companies shy away from asking employees to travel for work during the summer or on holidays, especially Mother's Day, Father's Day and Thanksgiving and Christmas. With corporate demand low then, hotels and conference centers discount their rooms. Again, expect to save 20 percent to 25 percent during off-peak times. **The most expensive months?** April, May, June, September and October, when demand is high.

WHEN IS THE BEST TIME FOR A BUSINESS OR COLLECTION AGENCY TO CONTACT ITS DEBTORS? Sixty-one days after the bill is due. Many businesses will give a customer 60 days to pay a bill before the calls begin. And studies show the longer it takes a customer to pay, the less he eventually will pay. A customer who owes, say, $1,000 is more likely to pay in full if he is contacted 61 to 75 days after he is contacted. After 90 days, he is less likely to pay in full, and after 180 days, he is very unlikely to repay his entire debt.

WHICH IS THE BEST MONTH FOR A BUSINESS TO PAY ITS BILLS? December. Whenever possible, prepay January and February bills in December, allowing you to count those expenses as a deduction on the current year's taxes. Consider prepaying rent, consultants, attorneys and others if you know what those costs will be, and use a company credit card so you can hold on to your cash until January. On the revenue side, defer as much income as you can until January so you don't have to record that as income until next year's tax return.

WHEN IS THE BEST TIME TO BUY OR LEASE COMMERCIAL REAL ESTATE? When the economy is bad. During these times, banks have foreclosed on a lot of property that they'd rather not own, and many people who own real estate have fallen on tough times and need to sell property. These two realities flood the commercial real estate market with buildings for sale, forcing banks and individuals to sell or lease property for less than they'd prefer. And that makes it a great time to buy or lease. As one broker said, "People have something, and they want it moved because they need the money." **Did you know?** Summer can be a very busy time for buying and leasing commercial real estate. Many businesses are slow in the summer and have time to plan a relocation. That explains why so many businesses move into new office space in the fall.

WHEN IS THE BEST TIME TO REVIEW THE INVESTMENT COMPANY THAT ADMINISTERS YOUR 401(K)? Once every three to five years, more often if your firm is growing fast. If not, five years might be often enough, but don't put it off any longer than that. Reviewing your plan provider allows you to get detailed information about how your plan's investments are doing and helps you stay on top of new Department of Labor rules regarding your responsibilities to your employees.

WHICH IS THE BEST MONTH TO MOVE YOUR COMPANY'S 401(K) PLAN FROM ONE INVESTMENT COMPANY TO ANOTHER? July or August. During the summer, human resources and financial staffs typically involved in these transfers tend to be less busy. Fewer plans are changing then and fewer mistakes are likely to be made when people are less likely to be overworked.

CHAPTER NINE

AROUND THE HOUSE

Have you ever heard this rule of thumb about home ownership? Set aside about 3 percent of the value of your house every year for housing expenses. So if your house is worth $200,000, prepare to spend $6,000 a year to repair it and enhance it. Even those of you who find yourselves in home-improvement stores every weekend might think you'd never spend that much money—until you stop and think about how much a new roof or new windows cost. But what if you knew the right time to buy things and do things to improve the look and condition of your house? I'm guessing you'd spend less than 3 percent. This chapter will give you lots of house-related tips to help you save time and money. They include the best time of year to have carpets professionally cleaned, hire a painter and replace your water heater; the best time of day to wash windows and vacuum; and the best month to have your roof replaced, hire a housekeeper, clean gutters and have your house appraised.

WHICH IS THE BEST MONTH TO HAVE A NEW ROOF PUT ON YOUR HOUSE AND SAVE A LOT OF MONEY? January or February, if you live in a place where snow and ice won't be an issue. Roofers have less work this time of year, giving the homeowner the upper hand when negotiating a price. The downside of working in cold weather, roofers say, could impact the quality of their work because, among other things, shingles are more brittle then and won't adhere to the roof as well.

WHEN IS THE BEST TIME OF THE YEAR TO HAVE A NEW ROOF PUT ON YOUR HOUSE AND EXPECT THE BEST JOB? Spring or fall. Shingles contain heat-activated sealant strips, which are designed to seal when they get hot. If you have your roof installed during the winter, the strips may not get hot enough for at least a few months. During the summer, it gets so hot on rooftops and shingles get so soft that installers can scar the shingles just by walking on them.

IF YOU ONLY CLEAN YOUR GUTTERS ONCE A YEAR, WHICH IS THE BEST MONTH TO DO IT? November. Cleaning your gutters in November, after the vast majority of leaves have fallen, prevents this worst-case scenario: the leaves and twigs block the downspouts, keeping gutters full of water, which freezes in the winter and causes your gutters to detach from the house. Clogged gutters can also lead to water damage to wood on the fascia boards and to other problems, including flooded basements. **What you can do:** Clean your gutters at least twice a year. May is another good time to rid your gutters of spring blossoms and "helicopters" from maple trees.

WHICH IS THE BEST TIME OF YEAR TO CLEAN YOUR GARAGE? Spring. Whether or not you park cars in your garage, spring is best. It's not too cold and not too warm, and that's important because cleaning out a garage can take several hours and very few are heated and cooled. If you park your cars in your garage, you'll want to mop or power wash the street salt and grime that falls from your cars onto the garage floor and wipe away the webs and nests from spiders and insects that used your garage for shelter when the weather turned cold. If you use your garage for storage, spring is a good time of year to decide what you want to keep and what should be thrown away or sold. Spring is also the most popular time of year for yard sales, so you won't need to store your "good junk" for too long before selling it.

WHICH IS THE BEST MONTH TO HIRE A GOOD HOUSEKEEPER? November or December. This is especially true if the economy is bad. With Christmas and Hanukkah approaching, some families try to cut their expenses and often decide to clean their houses themselves, letting the housekeeper go. That makes this a good time to find a sought-after housekeeper who otherwise wouldn't be available. Another reason why the November-December time frame works is you're more likely to have guests for holiday parties, and you'll want your house looking its best.

EVERYONE KNOWS HOUSEKEEPERS DON'T DO WINDOWS—CRUEL AND UNUSUAL PUNISHMENT?—SO IF YOU HAVE TO DO IT, WHEN IS THE BEST TIME TO WASH WINDOWS? Well, here's when you *shouldn't* do it: when it's windy outside or the sun is shining directly on the window. That's when you'll almost always see streaking. Evaporation happens faster during those times, and the window-washing fluid often will dry on the glass before you can wipe it off. **Tips:** Streaking can occur even if the weather conditions are perfect. Use quality window-washing fluid and not too little of it, and make sure your towels absorb liquid well. If you're using a squeegee, apply even pressure, whether you're moving it vertically or horizontally. And don't rush.

WHEN IS THE BEST TIME OF DAY TO VACUUM? Four p.m. Late afternoon is a great time of day to vacuum and do any other household cleaning chore. This is the time of day when we experience an energy boost, rebounding from the early afternoon when our bodies release chemicals that trigger sleepiness. Behavioral psychologists also say our moods are good in the late afternoon, and so the sight of a vacuum cleaner won't make us blue.

WHICH IS THE BEST TIME OF YEAR TO HAVE CARPETS PROFESSIONALLY CLEANED? Spring might be the obvious answer, but winter is a better time. Carpets dry faster because the cold, dry winter air sucks out the moisture, and heating systems, which lower humidity, also accelerate the drying process. Winter is the season when your family is indoors the most so it makes sense to want your carpets to be cleaner then. It's also the time when you can get the best deals. Carpet-cleaning companies are busiest during the spring and summer and before the end-of-the-year holiday season, when folks entertain and want their houses to look great and be their cleanest. Many companies offer discounts in January and February to get work in the door. **Second opinion:** Spring. If you're doing your spring cleaning anyway, why not have your carpets cleaned? If you choose spring, try to schedule the work for a day forecasted to be warm and dry. **What you can do:** Regardless of which season you choose, carpet-cleaning companies recommend doing a thorough cleaning at least every twelve to eighteen months.

IF YOU'RE MOVING INTO A HOUSE, WHEN IS THE BEST TIME TO HAVE CARPETS CLEANED? When the house is empty. Some people wait until after the movers bring in the furniture, assuming that they'll dirty the carpets during the course of doing their work. But moving companies cover at least the high-traffic areas of your carpet with runners. When the house is empty, the carpet-cleaning company can clean more square feet, and you'll get more for your money.

WHICH IS THE BEST TIME OF THE YEAR TO HIRE A PAINTER TO DO AN OUTDOOR JOB? During the winter. When it's cold outside and painters are doing indoor jobs, they're eager to line up warm-weather jobs, and they'll give you a good deal if you're willing to commit to them a few months in advance. It works the other way, too. **How about an indoor job?** Same principle. When the weather is warm and painters are working outdoors, hire someone to do an indoor job. The vast majority of them will be grateful to have work lined up so far into the future that they'll often give you a good deal. But even if they don't agree to do the work for less, you will have scheduled the work far in advance, and you'll be first in line when the weather turns cold.

WHEN IS THE BEST TIME OF DAY TO PAINT INDOORS? Start in the morning to give the room the greatest chance to ventilate before you go to sleep at night. Another reason to start painting then: the pros say they're sharpest in the morning and tend to make more mistakes as the day wears on. If they do, then you probably will, too. **Tip:** Whatever time you choose, paint when it's warm and dry outside. Very cold weather can cause condensation on windows, and that moisture can cause you to redo window frames. If it's raining, the moisture outside will extend drying time.

WHEN IS THE BEST TIME TO PAINT A NURSERY? Two months before the baby will use it. That will allow all the new-paint fumes to escape the room. Just to be safe, use nontoxic paints with low emissions.

WHICH IS THE BEST MONTH TO HAVE YOUR HOUSE APPRAISED IF YOU'RE REFINANCING AND YOU WANT A HIGH APPRAISAL? August or September. The housing market is most active during the spring and summer, so by the end of the summer housing values typically are at their highest level of the year, making it the best time to have your house appraised.

WHICH IS THE BEST MONTH TO HAVE YOUR HOUSE APPRAISED IF YOU'RE APPEALING A HIGH TAX BILL AND WANT A LOW APPRAISAL? February or March. Traditional slow sales in November, December, January and February mean appraisers will not be able to find many recent sales in your neighborhood to compare to your house. Those houses that do sell in the winter typically sell for less, as buyers take advantage of eager sellers. Lower sales prices will mean lower comps, helping your cause as you present your case to your local real estate appeal board.

WHICH IS THE BEST MONTH TO SIGN AN APARTMENT LEASE? December. Fewer people move in the winter than during any other season because the weather often is lousy and the days are shorter. In December, people have even less time because of holiday plans, and they have less money because they need to buy Christmas and Hanukkah gifts. This helps explain why apartment managers often offer the lowest rents and best deals of the year in December. **Tip:** People who are willing to move in December have the upper hand and should also ask for a free month's rent, a lower security deposit and a short-term lease.

WHICH IS THE BEST TIME OF THE MONTH TO GET THE ATTENTION OF YOUR HOME LOAN OFFICER? Early in the month and the middle of the month. Basically, any time but the end of the month, when a lot of real estate closings occur. Your loan officer doesn't have time then to talk, let alone start the process to get you a loan.

WHICH IS THE BEST TIME OF THE MONTH TO CLOSE ON A MORTGAGE? Two days before the end of the month. It's less stressful—and only a little more expensive—than closing on the last day of the month. Of course, everyone wants to close on the last day of the month because that's the cheapest day to close. Chances are your mortgage comes with a daily interest payment and if your interest payment is, say, $50 a day and you close on the twentieth of the month, you'll have to pay ten days of interest, or $500. If you wait until the last day of the month, you'll pay $50. Because so many people want to save a few bucks and close on the last day of the month, do yourself a favor and close the day before. You'll have a lot less stress.

WHEN IS THE BEST TIME TO REFINANCE YOUR MORTGAGE? When the housing market is experiencing a strong buyer's market. That almost always means the housing market is suffering badly, and the Federal Reserve won't want to do anything to make it worse. The Fed, which sets targets for short-term interest rates, will leave the rates alone because raising them would cause private banks to raise their rates, making it that much more difficult for people to afford to borrow money to buy houses. When the housing market is in the tank, banks send out millions of letters asking homeowners to refinance their mortgages. If it makes financial sense for you to do it, go ahead. Since 2010 homeowners have been saving hundreds of dollars per month, in some cases refinancing their mortgages with rates less than 4 percent. That represents historic lows.

WHICH IS THE BEST MONTH TO SIGN A CONTRACT TO HAVE A NEW HOUSE BUILT? In January, and preferably during a housing slump. Builders typically don't have a lot of work scheduled that month, and there aren't a lot of other people looking to start construction so early in the year. If the housing market is in the tank, builders are even more eager than usual to find work, and chances are interest rates on home loans are reasonable, so you can find an attractive mortgage.

WHICH IS THE BEST TIME OF THE YEAR TO REPLACE YOUR AIR-CONDITIONING SYSTEM? Fall and winter. Do it when you don't need it. Most people have their systems replaced in the spring and summer because they have to, so there's a big rush then. You don't want to be in a rush when it comes to replacing your AC unit. **What you can do:** Have your system checked out if it's older than ten years, especially if it's a lower-quality brand or if you had to have it repaired, especially to plug Freon leaks. That is often a sign that you'll need to replace your system before long.

WHEN IS THE BEST TIME TO REPLACE YOUR HEAT PUMP? When it's old but working well. Heat pumps typically last fifteen to twenty years, so if yours is getting close to that age, have it checked out. If you need to replace parts, ask your heating contractor how much time the new parts will buy you and then decide whether it makes more sense to just replace it. The worst-case scenario is that it will fail when you need it most. If that happens, you'll be at the mercy of your contractor, and you won't be in the best position to shop for the best price.

WHICH IS THE BEST TIME OF THE YEAR TO REPLACE YOUR WATER HEATER? Winter. You need hot water year-round, of course, but you arguably need it more in the winter. Cold showers are more bearable in the summer, no? Many plumbers say winter makes hot water heaters work harder. What better time to replace an old one with a new, more efficient one?

OK, SO THIS ONE IS AS MUNDANE AS THEY COME, BUT WHO WANTS TO PAY FOR WATER YOU'LL NEVER USE? WHEN IS THE BEST TIME TO REPLACE A WAX RING ON A COMMODE? Three times: (1) When the toilet is lifted off the flange for any reason. (2) When water is leaking from the base of the toilet. (3) When you see no water but your bathroom smells bad well after you flush. That wax ring, which costs only a couple of bucks, prevents leaks and keeps your bathroom from smelling like a horse stable. Leaking water and a foul smell are two signs that the ring is damaged. The ring's seal breaks whenever the toilet is removed, so don't try to save a couple of dollars by reusing a wax ring. You might be able to, but why risk it?

CHAPTER TEN

AROUND THE WORLD

Timing is incredibly important when it comes to travel. After all, how many tourists want to be in Anchorage in February or in Phoenix in July? A few of you, maybe, and the rest of you may wonder why you need a smarty-pants author to tell you to steer clear of Alaska in the winter and Arizona in the summer. But this chapter goes far beyond the obvious and includes lots of secrets and little-known tips from travel agents, concierges, hotel managers, airline executives and others. The facts you'll find here include the best time to use frequent-flier miles, the best time of the day to get the attention of a concierge, and the best months to drive cross-country, visit New York City if you're on a tight budget and travel to places as diverse as Hawaii, Beijing and Antarctica.

WHICH IS THE BEST TIME OF THE YEAR TO BOOK A HOTEL ROOM? The end of the quarter or the end of the year. Hotel sales staffers have quotas, just as car salesmen do, and they're usually quarterly quotas. So if you know you're taking a trip to a particular city sometime in the future, call a hotel you'd like to stay in at the end of March, June, September or December. Sales staffs become more eager to book rooms when the clock is ticking at the end of a quarter and bonuses are on the line. If you book a room then, regardless of when you actually stay at the hotel, it will count as a sale for the quarter when it is booked. **Tip:** If you're going to a city and you can be flexible about when you go, call hotels there and ask when they will offer discounted rates. Hotels know months in advance when they are likely to be busy and when they are likely to have plenty of vacancies. At the less busy times they'll offer the best rates. **Did you know?** Have you ever read an Internet review of a hotel you're interested in and wondered if it's real? A team from Cornell University has developed software that tries to spot fake positive reviews, and it claims an accuracy rate of nearly 90 percent—a 40-percentage-point improvement over discerning adults. The team found that true reviews more often use words that describe the hotel experience, such as bathroom, check-in and price, while fake reviews typically use words that explain why the alleged guest picked the hotel, such as business, vacation and husband.

WHEN IS THE BEST TIME OF DAY TO GET THE ATTENTION OF A HOTEL CONCIERGE? After 6 p.m. Before then, they're very busy helping hotel guests get tickets to plays or make restaurant reservations. The rush ends at about 6 p.m. After that, he or she will have plenty of time to hook you up with discount vouchers for museums and other attractions. Some even have discount vouchers for local department stores that can save you a mint. **What you can do:** Call your hotel the night before you arrive, ask for the concierge and tell him or her how excited you are to stay there. Ask for a restaurant suggestion just to build some rapport, and be sure to mention if your visit coincides with a birthday, anniversary or other special occasion. If you do, you may walk into your room and find a complimentary bottle of wine.

WHICH IS THE BEST MONTH TO DRIVE CROSS-COUNTRY? September. With the exception of an occasional hurricane making landfall in the Southeast, September offers some of the mildest and most pleasant weather from coast to coast. The northern part of the country won't have snow yet, and the southern part, including the deserts in the Southwest, will have cooled down. And that's a good thing for your vehicle, not to mention for you. Driving is easy in good weather, and if you can't afford to stay in hotels, sleeping in your car is bearable when the weather isn't too hot or cold. If you're not riding in an RV and you can afford hotels, most are less expensive after Labor Day, the unofficial end of summer. And parks and other tourist attractions, where you might want to stop along the way and spend some time, are less crowded starting in September. **What about traveling by train?** September, for all the same reasons. You can go from New York City to San Francisco in three and a half days on Amtrak. The path meanders a bit—it's 676 miles longer than the most direct highway route—but in between the large cities where the train stops, you'll see plenty of picturesque fields, forests, hills and mountains.

WHEN IS THE BEST TIME TO USE FREQUENT-FLIER AIRLINE MILES? When you fly Southwest. A consulting firm made 6,720 requests to redeem frequent-flier miles on twenty-four airline websites and was able to use the miles to get a free ticket 99.3 percent of the time when it went on Southwest's site. Only GOL, a low-fare carrier in Brazil, did better, allowing its frequent-flier miles to be used every time. After Southwest came Air Berlin, with a 96.4 percent success rate, followed by Virgin Australia (91.4 percent), Singapore (90.7 percent), Lufthansa (85 percent), Air Canada (82.1 percent) and JetBlue (79.3 percent). **The worst?** US Airways (25.7 percent), Delta (27.1 percent), Emirates (35.7 percent) and

AirTran (47.1 percent). **Did you know?** Unredeemed miles in all frequent-flier accounts worldwide total more than 9.7 *trillion*—enough miles to take 19.4 million round-trip trips to the moon. **And finally:** The price of a one-way ticket on America's first commercial flight, in 1914, was $5. The mayor of St. Petersburg paid that to go twenty-one miles, from St. Petersburg to Tampa. No word on how he returned to St. Petersburg.

THE CONSENSUS IS THAT TRAVEL INSURANCE OFTEN IS A WASTE OF MONEY, BUT SALES ARE WAY UP, SO WHEN IS THE BEST TIME TO BUY IT? When you're losing sleep over one of these possible trip-ending scenarios: a hurricane or other natural disaster, a serious illness, a missed flight, a loss of employment, a terrorist attack or civil unrest abroad. **Second opinion:** Those who say it's a waste of money point out that travel insurance often duplicates the coverage you have in homeowner's and health insurance and credit card policies and that most airlines will reimburse you for lost luggage regardless of whether you bought travel insurance. They also warn that travel insurance often comes with lots of exemptions and exclusions. **What you can do:** If you're going to buy it anyway, scour the Internet for the best prices, and know what your policy covers—and what it doesn't. If you want to play it safe, buy "cancel for any reason" coverage, though some airlines don't sell it. It will cost more—as much as 7.5 percent of the cost of your trip—but you'll have peace of mind.

IF YOU'RE TAKING A CRUISE, WHEN IS THE BEST TIME OF DAY TO GET A GREAT DEAL ON SPA TREATMENTS OR OTHER ONBOARD SERVICES? Late morning and early afternoon. Many cruise lines offer discounted services this time of day, when the ship is in port. When most of the passengers are off the ship, exploring a port city, the spas and shops are nearly empty. The ships hope these midday deals will keep some passengers on board for at least part of the day. Not surprisingly, the discounts aren't as deep when the weather is nasty and the cruise lines know that some passengers won't want to brave bad weather.

WHEN IS THE BEST TIME TO WAKE UP IN THE DAYS BEFORE TRAVELING FROM THE UNITED STATES TO EUROPE? Early, earlier and earlier still. In an attempt to reset your body clock, one researcher recommends travelers rise at 6 a.m. two days before the trip, at 5 a.m. on the day before the trip and at 3 a.m. on the day of the trip. Assuming it's a late-afternoon flight, travelers, who are likely to be pretty tired by then, should try to sleep on the plane, avoiding meals, drinks and movies.

WHICH IS THE BEST TIME OF DAY TO GO TO THE TOP OF THE SEARS TOWER, THE LARGEST BUILDING IN THE WESTERN HEMISPHERE? Well, technically you can't go to the top of the 110-story building in Chicago—the observation deck is on the 103rd floor. But the best time for the observation deck is when it opens, at 9 a.m. from April through September, or at 10 a.m. from October through March. Relatively few people venture to the observation deck then, even on clear, sunny days, when hoards of people will wait till later in the day to take in the view, which allows you to see four states: Indiana, Michigan, Wisconsin and, of course, Illinois. First thing in the morning is also the best time to go to the observation deck of the Empire State Building in New York City. Of course, lines are much shorter at the Sears Tower and at the Empire State Building on rainy, overcast days, but there isn't nearly as much to see on those days, and the nicest cashiers will talk you out of buying a ticket then. **Did you know?** The Sears Tower is now officially named the Willis Tower, for the building's owner Willis Group Holdings, a London-based insurance company.

WHICH IS THE BEST MONTH TO VISIT NEW YORK CITY IF YOU'RE ON A BUDGET? January. After New Year's, when the hoards of holiday visitors have left the city, you can get great rates on airfare and at Manhattan hotels. It's also much easier to get restaurant reservations and theater tickets, and post-Christmas sales at department stores offer deep discounts on clothes and other items you may not be able to find elsewhere. True, it can be bitter cold and snowy then, but it can be bitter and cold and snowy a lot of places in the world in January. Pack your wool garments, bundle up and enjoy yourself.

WHICH IS THE BEST MONTH TO VISIT HAWAII? May or October. These two months—and the latter half of April and to a lesser extent September and November—are when you can get the best deals on hotels and airfare and when there are fewer tourists. May and October are also two of the best weather months of the year. High season, when everything typically costs more, is from mid-December to mid-April, and the summer months are the most crowded and sometimes uncomfortably hot. **What you can do:** If you choose to go in the late spring, remember that the end of April and beginning of May is Japanese Golden Week, when many thousands of Japanese go to Hawaii. And if you want to go in January or February, make reservations far in advance because that's when a lot of Americans go. **Did you know?** Hilo, Hawaii, receives an annual average rainfall of 126.27 inches, making it the rainiest city in America. The sunniest city, by the way, is Yuma, Arizona, which receives only 3.01 inches a year. Yuma's daily newspaper is, of course, the *Yuma Sun.*

WHICH IS THE BEST MONTH TO VISIT JUNEAU, ALASKA? May. Sure, it's warmer during the summer, but May isn't too cold, and it doesn't rain as much then, and the tourists, many of whom arrive by cruise ship, don't arrive en masse until June, July and August. Avoid September and October, Juneau's rainiest months. **Tip:** May isn't rainy by Juneau standards, but the city sees a lot of rain year-round—it rains 222 days a year—and can also be very windy. Bring a raincoat with a hood and leave your umbrella at home, as the locals do.

WHICH IS THE BEST MONTH TO SKI IN COLORADO? January. Wait until the middle of the month and the snow will be deep but the slopes won't be too crowded. With Christmas in the rearview mirror, most people don't have a lot of cash to spend on skiing. Many resorts try to lure locals to the slopes in January with midweek discounts on lift passes. **Second opinion:** April, as long as you're there after the spring break crowds leave. It's the warmest month during the ski season, but the occasional April blizzard makes for good skiing well into the month. The snow might get a bit soft and slushy in Vail and Beaver Creek but not in Loveland and some of the higher elevation resort towns. Skiing is also cheaper after spring break and cheaper still if you go Sunday through Thursday. **The worst times?** Around Thanksgiving, Christmas, Presidents' Day weekend and spring break.

WHICH IS THE BEST MONTH TO HANG GLIDE OFF THE DUNES IN KITTY HAWK OR ELSEWHERE IN THE OUTER BANKS OF NORTH CAROLINA? May or October. The world's longest running hang gliding competition, the Hang Gliding Spectacular, occurs during the second half of May. The four-day event—the first one happened in 1973—is intended to get people interested in hang gliding. In May, the weather is great and most of the tourists haven't descended upon the Outer Banks, so hotel rates are reasonable and rates for rental houses are about a third of what they'll be in the middle of the summer. Many hang gliders—even those who participate in the Hang Gliding Spectacular—insist that the fall offers the most "soarable" conditions, when swirling fall winds keep them aloft longer than any other time of the year. Because the prime tourist season there is roughly from Memorial Day to Labor Day, October visitors also pay less for lodging and see fewer people on the dunes as well as on the nearby beaches.

WHICH IS THE BEST MONTH TO SCUBA DIVE IN THE CARIBBEAN? April. Of course, if you talk with enough divers, you'll hear about wonderful dives they've had during every month of the year. But here's a case for April: first, rainfall is low in April throughout the Caribbean, and that almost always means visibility is high. Less rain means less rainwater washing soil into the sea. After April, the rains pick up through the end of hurricane season on November 30. That doesn't mean there aren't wonderful days to dive between May 1 and November 30—there are—but most divers would rather enter the water during a dry spell. Second, with few storms in April, the sea is often calm. Third, the air temperature is pleasant, as is the water temperature. Finally, the peak tourism season ends in mid-April, so if you go during the latter half of the month, you'll save on airfare and lodging.

WHICH IS THE BEST MONTH TO VISIT VIRGINIA BEACH? September. While it's true that September is peak hurricane season along the Atlantic, it's unlikely you'll actually experience one. What's likely is you'll get pleasant beach weather, with high temperatures in the low 80s. And by September, the summer crowds are gone, and hotel rates have plummeted. Snag an oceanfront room at a hotel that offers a complimentary breakfast for less than $100 a day.

WHICH IS THE BEST TIME OF THE YEAR TO VISIT WASHINGTON, D.C.? Fall. Much of the humidity and most of the tourists are gone, making the city much more comfortable and much less crowded. The hotels lower their prices not long after Labor Day, and the city's leafy parks display beautiful colors in October. **A second opinion:** Spring, largely because of the spectacular cherry trees that line the Tidal Basin near the Jefferson Memorial, and which bloom in March and April. **The worst time?** Summer. Tourists outnumber residents, which means the attractions are crowded and most people can't give you directions when you ask for them. Hotel rates are high in the summer, and the city can seem like it's in the Deep South because it gets incredibly hot and humid, especially in July and August.

WHICH IS THE BEST MONTH TO SEE THE SUPREME COURT HEAR A CASE? January or February. If you just want to see the court in action and don't care which case you hear, winter is the best time because it gives you the best chance to hear a case. The weather typically isn't good in Washington, D.C., then, and fewer tourists and locals are willing to wait outside the Supreme Court building in the cold, so the lines are shorter, giving you a better chance to get inside. **The worst month?** April. This is the last month of the session that the Court has "argument days"—hearings that are open to the public—and Court enthusiasts who haven't made it to a hearing by then will line up by the hundreds early in the morning, making it less likely that you'll get to hear an entire argument. There is, however, a separate line for people who are content to enter the courtroom and listen for just a few minutes before they are ushered out. **What you can do:** Check the Supreme Court's website, http://www.supremecourt.gov, to see the schedule. When you're inside, common sense prevails: Be quiet. Don't take photographs. And you can't smoke, drink or eat in the courtroom. Just like any courthouse.

WHICH IS THE BEST TIME OF THE YEAR TO VISIT MEXICO CITY? Easter week. This is when a lot of Mexicans and Mexico City residents are off work and schools are closed, so they tend to travel to their hometowns or to one of the coasts. At this time, there is less traffic in the city than you'll see the rest of the year, and there is less smog. With fewer Mexicans in the city, the attractions aren't swamped, and hotel rooms aren't hard to find. If Easter week coincides with your children's spring break, it's a great time to go. **How about Cabo San Lucas?** March. It rarely rains in March in this west coast city, and the temperatures usually rise to the low 80s. If you go in March, just make sure it's not spring break week. College students in the West who go to Cabo turn it into a wild party city, and they drive up hotel rates then.

WHEN IS THE BEST TIME TO VISIT THE AMAZON RAIN FOREST? If you don't like rain, there's never a great time to go. It rains a lot in the Amazon, especially from December to May, but it's less rainy from July through September. As with the Everglades, that means there are fewer mosquitoes in the summer, and it's a good time to fish and swim. Reasons not to go in the summer: it's hot, and after the rainy season, vegetation clogs some waterways. Except for aquatic life, wildlife is harder to spot. If you don't mind some rain, October and November and May and June are cooler.

WHICH IS THE BEST MONTH TO VISIT BEIJING? September or October. The weather is pleasant then, unlike the hot and humid summers and the bitter cold and snowy winters. By early fall, the attractions are easier to see without the hoards of Chinese and international tourists who descend on Beijing in June, July and August. Hotel rooms are not only easier to book in the fall, but they're cheaper then, too, as are international flights to Beijing. The exception to the September-October rule is the first week of October. The Chinese celebrate National Day on October 1, and workers take off a few days sometime between then and October 8 or 9. Beijing is often their destination, and hoteliers and restaurateurs there often jack up prices to take advantage of the influx of Chinese tourists.

WHICH IS THE BEST MONTH TO VISIT NEW ZEALAND? February. New Zealand has become a travel hot spot for North Americans and Asians, and people who love it say there isn't a bad time to visit. It's true that the weather, especially on the North Island, is relatively mild year-round. But here's a case for February: December, January and February—summer in New Zealand—are the warmest months by far, with low temperatures in the upper 50s and highs in the mid to upper 80s. But international tourists pour into New Zealand in December and January, when New Zealanders themselves become tourists in their own country. Kiwi families tend to get a lot of time off school and work from mid-December through the end of January, making it hard to find hotel rooms at beach destinations. December and January also are the two most expensive months to stay in and fly to New Zealand, unless you arrive before December 9. Those who like skiing in the summer—New Zealand's winter, in June, July and August—should expect to pay a premium to stay in ski lodges and resorts. **A second opinion:** Those who don't mind being there during some chilly nights and days love New Zealand during the late spring or early fall. **Money-saving tip:** When planning a trip to New Zealand, it usually pays to buy your airline tickets as early as possible.

WHICH IS THE BEST MONTH TO VISIT THE GALAPAGOS ISLANDS? April or May. That's still the rainy season, but it rains only about two inches per month during the rainy season, and the rainy season, believe it or not, is a time of the year when the Galapagos also gets a lot of sun. In April and May, the waters remain warm and the ocean is calm, making swimming and snorkeling a more comfortable experience. In late spring, tortoises are active and sea lions are feisty as they look for mates. Flowers are blossoming, and much of the place looks lush and green. Also, it's a bit cheaper to stay there then compared with the peak seasons—from mid-June to early September and from mid-December to mid-January. **A second opinion:** If you're going to the Galapagos Islands to scuba dive or snorkel, you'll want to go in the summer or fall. Starting in June, ocean currents bring cold water, but they also bring lots of plankton and nutrients, which attract lots of fish and penguins. So if you can brave the cold waters, the latter half of the year is the best time to see incredible fish and other marine life.

WHEN IS THE BEST TIME TO TAKE A CRUISE SHIP VACATION IN EUROPE? Here's a summary: **The Mediterranean:** Spring and fall, when it's not so hot in Greece, Turkey, Italy and Spain. **Scandinavia and the Baltics:** Late May to early September. That's when cruise lines usually go to northern Europe. (You can take a ferry year-round along the coast of Norway.) The best weather there is in late summer, but mid-June to early July is an interesting time to go because of the midnight sun, which only disappears for three to four hours each night. **Great Britain:** Late summer and early fall. It's the sunniest then, but it's cooler—with high temperatures in the 60s—than on the European continent. **The largest rivers:** Fall. Tours of the largest rivers occur from early spring through November, and summer has the best weather, but the fall colors are incredible, and the temperatures are comfortable then. "Tulip cruises" operate in the Netherlands from March through mid-May, with tulips at their best in April. **The Atlantic Islands, Portugal and western France:** Fall. Cruise ships often visit Madeira and the Canary Islands and ports in Portugal and western France in the spring and fall. The weather is good throughout the year, but it's more likely to rain in the spring.

WHEN IS THE BEST TIME TO VISIT ZANZIBAR? July. This is the middle of the winter in Zanzibar, which consists of two islands off the east coast of Tanzania, in the Indian Ocean. Once the center of the Arab slave trade, Zanzibar, population 1.1 million, is becoming a hot spot for European and African tourists who love sunbathing on its wide beaches and snorkeling in its coral reefs. Zanzibar is warm year-round, but December, January and February are a bit too warm for some, March to June is the rainy season, August is the coolest month and September to November is also rainy.

WHEN IS THE BEST TIME TO VISIT CAPE TOWN? November to March. The Southern Hemisphere's summer months are the best time to hit this South Africa city's great beaches for swimming and surfing. Another big draw is the Cape Town area vineyards, which produce some of the best wines in the world.

WHEN IS THE BEST TIME TO SEE VICTORIA FALLS? March to May. This is the rainy season in southern Africa, when about five hundred million quarts of water at any one time fall into the Zambezi River, forming a curtain of water that is 355 feet high and more than a mile wide inside two national parks—Mosi-oa-Tunya National Park in Zambia and Victoria Falls National Park in Zimbabwe. The water generates spray that shoots a thousand feet high and can be seen thirty miles away. That explains the name Mosi-oa-Tunya, which translates to smoke that thunders.

TOURISTS HAVE BEEN GOING TO ANTARCTICA FOR THREE DECADES. WHICH IS THE BEST MONTH TO GO? February. It's not as warm as January, but February is the best month for whale watching, and it's also the best month to see newly born penguin chicks frolicking. Because February is toward the end of the continent's summer cruise ship season, you might find cheaper rates than you would in December or January. The mildest weather in Antarctica is on the Antarctic Peninsula and along the coastlines, where high temperatures range from the teens to the low 30s in the summer months of December, January and February. The coldest weather is on the South Pole as well as in higher elevations in eastern Antarctica. **Did you know?** Antarctica only receives about six or seven inches of snow a year, but the blizzards are fierce because the snow never melts and high winds viciously blow it around. The lowest temperature ever recorded on Earth—minus 128.6 degrees Fahrenheit—was in Antarctica on July 21, 1983. The highest temperature recorded in Antarctica? 58.3 degrees Fahrenheit, on January 5, 1974.

WHEN IS THE BEST TIME TO LET YOUR FACEBOOK FRIENDS KNOW ABOUT YOUR VACATION? After you return. You should always assume bad guys will figure out a way to read your Facebook posts. Fifteen percent of Facebook users tempt burglars by letting the world know about their travel plans in advance or by posting photos of their families while on vacation. **Tip:** Make your house look lived in while you're away. Leave inexpensive toys in your front yard and a car in your driveway, if possible, and, of course, leave some lights on in your house.

CHAPTER ELEVEN

AROUND THE KITCHEN

Traveling is a wonderful thing, but we can live without it. We can't live without eating and drinking, though, so here are some timing tips related to food and drink. You'll learn the best time of day to eat lunch and to eat a doughnut and the best time to drink wine, start eating at a dinner party and consume spicy food. We'll start off with something just about everyone eats—or should eat.

WE TYPICALLY GET THE MOST NUTRITIONAL VALUE FROM EATING VEGETABLES RAW, BUT WHEN IS IT BEST TO COOK THEM? Heating tomatoes, carrots and spinach actually brings out the best in them, releasing certain nutrients, including antioxidants. Use pressure cookers, steamers and microwaves whenever possible because they tend to keep the vitamins and nutrients where they belong. Boiling robs vegetables of the most vitamins and nutrients, which end up in the water. And, remember, using oil and butter to cook veggies adds fat and calories to them.

WHEN IS THE BEST TIME OF DAY TO EAT LUNCH? At 11 a.m. *and* 2 p.m. A growing number of doctors and nutritionists advocate eating four smaller meals a day rather than the traditional three meals. They urge their patients to eat a big breakfast, a small dinner and two three-hundred-calorie lunches—an early lunch to raise your blood sugar and fire up your metabolism and a later lunch to boost your energy and combat early-afternoon sleepiness, the result of a dip in body temperature. **What you can do:** Here are some suggestions for your two low-calorie lunches: a peanut butter pita, a small turkey wrap with cheese and lettuce, fruit with either low-fat yogurt or cottage cheese.

WHEN IS THE BEST TIME OF THE DAY TO EAT A DOUGHNUT? In the morning, if that's all you have. The American Dietetic Association doesn't advocate the consumption of doughnuts, but it says eating breakfast is so important that it's better to eat a doughnut for breakfast than nothing at all. The doughnut will provide a sugar boost to give you energy for an hour or two as you start your day. **What you can do:** Of course, just about anything else has more nutritional value than a doughnut. Plenty of studies show that protein-rich foods, such as eggs, yogurt and lean meat, and fiber-rich foods, such as whole wheat bread, whole-grain cereals and fruits, will help you feel full longer. A 2010 study showed that men who ate eggs in the morning not only felt full longer than men who ate bagels, but they took in fewer calories during the next twenty-four hours than the bagel eaters. **Did you know?** We sometimes don't think of fruit when we're looking for more fiber in our diets, but some of the most common fruits are rich in fiber. Try apples, bananas, kiwis, oranges, pears, prunes and berries.

IF THE MORNING IS THE BEST TIME TO EAT THE BIGGEST MEAL OF THE DAY, WHAT'S THE WORST TIME?
Right before bed. Most people assume this has to do with burning calories, but that's not true. Your body actually burns calories when you're in bed, but studies show it's harder to sleep while your body is digesting food. **Tip:** Not only should you refrain from eating right before bedtime, but eating spicy food makes it even more difficult to sleep because of the indigestion and heartburn that sometimes follow.

WHEN IS THE BEST TIME TO EAT SPICY FOOD? When it's very hot outside. Hot, spicy food will cause you to sweat, and that helps your body cool off by lowering your body temperature. It's the same logic behind flu sufferers: fevers are good because it's a sign that the body is fighting an infection, and when the fever results in sweating, it reduces your body temperature.

WHICH IS THE BEST DAY OF THE WEEK TO BUY BREAD? The day it's delivered to your local dollar store. More and more dollar stores are selling bread for as little as a third of what you'll pay at a grocery store, and often the bread won't go bad until ten days or more after it arrives at the store. Save on trips to your dollar store and buy a few loaves at a time. Freeze the ones you won't use right away.

WHICH IS THE BEST MONTH TO BUY DISPOSABLE PLATES, CUPS AND PLASTIC FORKS AND SPOONS?
May. This is the beginning of picnic season, and it's during or just before lots of high school and college graduation parties. Grocery stores and other retailers know most of us aren't serving our guests on those occasions with our finest china—or any china for that matter. You'll find sales on disposable party supplies as stores try to get you in the door so you'll buy lots of full-priced items that you never intended to buy. Same goes for ketchup,

mustard, relish and other picnic-related items. Isn't that in some book called *Buy Ketchup in May and Fly at Noon*?

WHEN IS THE BEST TIME TO START EATING AT A DINNER PARTY? After everyone has been served, if it's a party of, say, four to eight people. It's considered uncouth to eat before everyone has been served. Don't do it even if the host or hostess tells you it's OK. It's not. If it's a larger dinner party, say, ten to sixteen guests, it is fine to start eating if the hostess encourages you to do so. And if the gathering is larger than that, feel free to start if people near you have been served and have begun to eat. If it's a large, buffet-style gathering, all the women, except maybe the hostess, should get in line before the men, and you may start eating as soon as you sit down.

WHEN IS THE BEST TIME TO START COOKING AFTER FIRING UP A GAS GRILL? After ten to fifteen minutes. A lot of people don't realize it, but gas grills can take longer to heat up than charcoal grills, and preheating is just as important in your backyard as it is in your kitchen. **Did you know?** Americans spend an average of thirty minutes per day cooking while Indians and Turks spend the most time of anyone in the world—seventy-four minutes per day on average.

SPEAKING OF BARBECUING, WHEN IS THE BEST TIME TO TAKE STEAK OUT OF THE REFRIGERATOR BEFORE GRILLING IT? Thirty minutes before cooking it. If you do that, it will brown better and cook more evenly, and a steak prepared rare will never be cold in the center. **Tip:** Don't season steak until right before you cook it. The salt or other seasoning may dry out the meat a bit if you season ahead of time.

WHEN IS THE BEST TIME TO CUT STEAK OR OTHER RED MEAT YOU'VE GRILLED? Five to ten minutes after you take it off the grill. If you cut steak right after it comes off the grill, much of the juice in the meat will pour out of it. If you wait five to ten minutes, you'll give the juice time to absorb into the meat, keeping it more moist as you eat it. **Tip:** Don't use a barbecue fork when you're grilling. Piercing chicken, steaks or bratwurst will release the juices inside them and cause them to dry out. Piercing is okay to do with hot dogs because they're precooked.

WHEN IS THE BEST TIME TO BRUSH SWEET BARBECUE SAUCE ON CHICKEN AS YOU GRILL IT? A few minutes before you're ready to take it off the grill. Otherwise, the sugar in the sauce will burn and blacken the skin of the chicken, perhaps giving you the impression that it's done when, in fact, the inside of the chicken is red and undercooked. **Tip:** If grease gets on your wood deck, spray it with oven cleaner, then wash it with soapy water before you hose it off.

WHEN IS THE BEST TIME TO COOK CHICKEN AFTER DEFROSTING IT? Right away. This gives you the best chance to kill harmful bacteria that chickens pick up after pecking at droppings or drinking contaminated water. Cook the chicken to at least 165 degrees, and refrigerate or freeze leftovers within two hours after cooking. **Did you know?** In 2011, the U.S. Department of Agriculture broke with a decades-long guideline and said pork should be cooked to 145 degrees, not 160 degrees.

WHEN IS THE BEST TIME TO UNCORK A BOTTLE OF WINE AFTER YOU BUY IT? It depends, but here's a rule of thumb: if it's an inexpensive bottle—say, $10 or less—it's probably meant to be drunk within a year. More expensive wines, including Bordeauxs and Barolos, are meant to sit in a cellar or a wine rack for at least five years. This isn't always the case (excuse the pun). Sometimes inexpensive wine, especially reds, benefits from a few years in a cellar, and sometimes expensive wine is meant to be drunk soon after it's bought. **Tip:** If you want to know for sure, ask someone you trust at your local wine shop.

WHEN IS THE BEST TIME TO START DRINKING WINE AFTER YOU OPEN THE BOTTLE? At least fifteen minutes after you open it. Wine that mixes with the air, also known as aerating, gets a chance to smell and taste more like the winemaker intended. Red wines, with high tannin levels, typically need more time to breathe. A young cabernet sauvignon, for example, would benefit from one hour of breathing. **Tip:** Just uncorking or unscrewing the bottle isn't enough to allow it to breathe. Pour the wine into a decanter or into glasses. Otherwise, only the surface of the wine will aerate.

CHAPTER TWELVE

AROUND THE YARD

D on't have a green thumb? Don't worry about it. Whether you work at a botanical garden or own a lonely potted plant on a high-rise balcony, there's something in this chapter for you. Read on to learn the best time of day to mow your lawn, apply weed killer and pick strawberries; the best month to buy flowers and plant annuals; and the best time of the year to spread mulch, plant azaleas and prune trees.

WHEN IS THE BEST TIME TO BUY BUSHES AND TREES? The fall. Prices plummet starting around Labor Day as nurseries try to get rid of their stock before chilly weather sets in and no one wants to spend time in their yards. Fall also is a great time to buy bulbs, some of which can be planted right away while others will store well until the spring. **What you can do:** Make sure you know how to store bulbs. Some are temperature sensitive and may die during the winter if they're stored in cold garages and toolsheds.

HOW ABOUT THE BEST MONTH TO BUY FLOWERS AND PLANTS? August. They have a shorter shelf life, so they typically go on sale a couple of weeks before Labor Day. You'll want to plant them ASAP. **What you can do:** Warehouse stores—and to a lesser extent, big-box retailers—charge a lot less for flowers, bushes and trees than do garden supply stores and nurseries. Of course, their selection isn't as good, but expect to save as much as 50 percent by buying those plants at warehouse stores during prime planting season.

GARDEN TOOLS? Spring. Garden supply stores and home improvement stores stock gardening tools year-round, so they won't try to dump them in the fall, as they do plants. You'll find good deals in the spring as these stores offer discounts on rakes, weeders and shovels in March and April to try to lure you into their stores, where they hope you'll buy full-price flowers and plants at high-profit-margin prices. **Tip:** The cliché you get what you pay for is especially true for garden tools. If you're hard on your shovels and rakes, spend a little more, and they'll last for many years.

WHEN IS THE BEST TIME OF DAY TO MOW THE LAWN? Late afternoon or early evening. Unless it just rained, the morning dew has long since dried and the grass is dry, making it easier to handle the clippings. What's more, most of us—thanks to our body clocks—get a boost of energy in the late afternoon, and that also makes this job easier. **Did you know?** This boost of energy also helps explain why late afternoon is the best time of day to clean your house.

WHEN IS THE BEST TIME TO TUNE UP YOUR LAWN MOWER? After about fifty hours of use or once a season, whichever comes first. Or more often than that if you mow in extreme heat, in a dusty field or you mostly cut tall, wet grass. If you don't do any of those things, once a year probably is enough. An annual tune-up almost always will include changing an air filter, sharpening blades, replacing oil and cleaning out the gas tank. It's only necessary to replace spark plugs after about one hundred hours of use. **Did you know?** Old, stale gasoline is often the cause of sluggish performance. Whenever possible, use gasoline that is no more than a month old.

IF YOU COULD ONLY DO IT ONCE A YEAR, WHICH IS THE BEST MONTH TO APPLY WEED AND FEED TO YOUR LAWN? April. April is sort of in the middle of spring, as far as most landscapers are concerned. It's around the time when lawns are waking up for the year and when they're busy using the energy they stored when temperatures turned cold. Throughout most of the country, weed and feed works best then, after the first frost and when weeds are growing. Apply it to a lawn that was cut two to four days earlier, and preferably after it rains so the weed and feed will stick to the leaves of the weeds. Most weed-and-feed products also work best when it's at least 70 degrees Fahrenheit, but don't apply it too far into May. Your lawn will get fed, but it won't have much effect on the weeds. By late spring, mature weeds scoff at weed and feed.

WHEN IS THE BEST TIME OF DAY TO APPLY WEED KILLER? In the morning if it's a granular weed killer, and around noon or in the early afternoon if it's liquid. The dampness of the morning dew helps the granular weed killer stick to the weeds, making the weed killer more effective. Spraying the liquid weed killer around noon means the weed will probably be dry and better able to absorb the liquid, which is especially effective when it's hot and sunny.

WHICH IS THE BEST TIME OF THE YEAR TO SPREAD MULCH? Late spring. You'll want to wait until after the soil has warmed. Any earlier and you will keep the soil from warming as soon as it should and you could delay plant growth. **Second opinion:** If you live in the Deep South, Texas or the Southwest, you may want to spread mulch earlier in the spring, before a lot of weeds emerge. Spreading mulch over certain weeds will kill them before they reach the surface. **Tip:** There's no need to move the mulch when you apply fertilizer. Just put the fertilizer on top; water will move the nutrients down to the roots.

WHICH IS THE BEST TIME OF THE YEAR TO HAVE YOUR SOIL TESTED? Fall. By then the soil will have reacted with fertilizer, lime and whatever else you put on it during spring and summer. A soil test will help you figure out what your plants need. Plus, submitting soil samples in fall gives you plenty of time to prepare your beds by the time you start planting in spring. (Winter isn't a good time because soil samples are less reliable when the ground is frozen.) **Tip:** Test your soil every three to five years unless you need to add a lot of limestone and fertilizer. If that's the case, have your soil tested a year after you do that.

WHICH IS THE BEST MONTH TO PLANT ANNUALS? April. This is true for most of the lower forty-eight states, though it might be a good idea to wait until May if you live in the extreme north. The key is planting after the last frost of winter. Most annuals don't survive frost, unlike perennials, which tend to be heartier and can be planted as early as March and also in the fall. **What you can do:** If you buy your annuals and aren't sure about whether you'll get another frost, put them outside but keep them in their containers and water them during the day, and then move them into the garage at night. They'll grow and strengthen in their pots until they get planted.

WHICH ARE THE BEST DAYS OF THE YEAR TO PLANT TULIPS, CROCUSES OR OTHER FLOWER BULBS? Columbus Day, Halloween and Veterans Day. There's no specific link between these holidays and planting bulbs, but you'll want to plant your bulbs right before the first frost of the season, and depending on where you live, these holidays are near the first frost. Because they are holidays, it's easier to associate bulbs with these days than with random days in October and November. And you may be off work on Columbus Day and Veterans Day, making them a great time to get out into the garden and plant. Planting your bulbs in October or early November will allow them to rest in the cold ground for several weeks, as they need to do, before they erupt in the spring. **Tips:** Plant bulbs deeper than you would seed, but make sure they don't have to fight through soil packed with clay. Even the heartiest perennials have trouble around clay. Although it's best to plant bulbs right before the first frost, you can plant them after the first frost as long as the ground can be worked easily. **Did you know?** Some gardeners say you can put bulbs in your refrigerator or freezer during the winter, plant them in March and trick them into sprouting in the spring.

WHICH IS THE BEST TIME OF THE YEAR TO PLANT AZALEAS? Early spring or early fall, when the ground is cool. Make sure the soil is loose, drains well and is fertilized. New azalea bushes need a lot of water, so if you live in a dry climate, water them at least once a week for as long as a year.

WHICH IS THE BEST TIME OF THE YEAR TO PLANT PINE SAPLINGS? Spring. The cool, moist ground gives the young plants the best chance to survive. Before you plant them, keep them in a cool, damp place and when you plant them, make sure the roots are moist. The roots are so fragile that if they're exposed to the sun and wind for only ten minutes, they may die.

WHEN IS THE BEST TIME TO CUT DOWN A TREE THAT YOU WANT TO USE FOR FIREWOOD? Winter, before the air temperature warms up and the release of sap makes cutting more difficult. After you fell the tree, you'll want the wood to air-dry for at least six to eight months, during which time the tree will lose about 20 percent of its moisture. For the airing-out process to work best, you'll need to cut and split the wood, and this works best when it is frozen. If you cut down a tree in January, you can burn that wood by the following January. **Did you know?** Dried-out firewood produces 7,700 BTU of energy when burned, and green, wet wood produces only 5,000 BTU. Not only that, but dried-out wood burns easier.

WHICH IS THE BEST TIME OF THE YEAR TO PRUNE MOST TREES? Winter. You want to prune when the tree is dormant. Pruning is less stressful for the tree when it's not growing, and pruning in the winter gives trees time to heal before the growing season. You also don't have to worry about insect infestation then, which is particularly important to trees such as birches and American elms. Winter pruning also makes it easier for the pruner, who can see better without leaves in the way. **The worst time?** Late spring and early summer, when trees are putting their energy into growing. Pruning trees then shocks them. Exceptions to this rule: some trees and bushes can be pruned in the summer after they've bloomed. Here are several of the exceptions: azaleas, flowering crabapples, forsythias, big-leaf hydrangeas, lilacs, magnolias, mock oranges and rhododendrons. **Tip:** If you have very light pruning to do or if you need to remove dead branches, it really doesn't matter when you do it. Not sure if a branch is dead? Scratch it. If you see green under the bark, it's alive.

HOW ABOUT PRUNING FRUIT TREES? The key to pruning fruit trees, like other kinds of trees, is knowing when the pruning will stress out the trees the least and promote the most growth. **Apples and pears–**Late winter, **Apricots–**Late summer, **Plums, peaches and nectarines–**Midsummer, **Cherries–**Early summer, **Citrus–**After the fruit is picked.

WHEN IS THE BEST TIME OF DAY TO PICK STRAWBERRIES? Between 6 a.m. and 8 a.m., when they're cool and the plants are stronger. If you have plants in your garden, pick strawberries every other day, or three days a week, to give them a break and lessen the stress caused by harvesting the fruit. When you harvest, pick the reddest ones and leave a quarter of the stem attached. That keeps them fresher longer.

WHEN IS THE BEST TIME OF DAY TO SPRAY FOR ADULT MOSQUITOES? At dusk, when they're the most active, looking for food—your blood. When they're hunting for food, mosquitoes are exposed and most vulnerable to spray. The exception—sorry to say—is the Asian tiger mosquito, which lives throughout the Southeast and in recent years has crept into the Midwest and Northeast. These nasty critters feed during the day, and, unfortunately, are more aggressive than other species and don't go down without a fight. Some traps that emit carbon dioxide work against the tiger mosquitoes, which have been in the United States since at least 1985. **What you can do:** If you get a mosquito bite, apply ice or anti-itch lotions or take Benadryl, all of which reduce inflammation. Toothpaste also helps, as long as it contains menthol.

CHAPTER THIRTEEN

AROUND THE KENNEL

Sixty-two out of one hundred households in America own at least one pet, and if you count fish, there are more pets (377 million) than people (312 million) in the United States. We spend about $51 billion a year on these critters—$22 billion more than just ten years ago, when most of us had more disposable income. More than 90 percent of pet owners consider their pets to be members of their families, and two out of three Americans say they wouldn't vote for a presidential candidate who didn't like pets. OK, so it's pretty clear that we love our pets, and what's not to love? As nineteenth-century British author George Eliot said, "Animals are such agreeable friends. They ask no questions; they pass no criticisms." Eliot would devour this chapter, which includes tips on the best time of day to go to the vet, ride a horse and catch a runaway hamster or gerbil; the best time of year to buy a dog or a cat; and the best time to spay or neuter a dog, potty train a puppy and buy pet insurance.

WHICH IS THE BEST TIME OF THE YEAR TO BUY A DOG OR CAT? Summer. This is the time of year when most people have the most free time, and that's the key—giving your pet as much of your time as you can. Pets, especially puppies and kittens, need guidance, training and attention, and they're more likely to get it when their owners are not in school or are spending less time at work.

WHEN IS THE BEST TIME IN A CAT'S LIFE TO BUY ONE? When it's an adult. Its personality is developed, so you know what you're getting when you first meet it and spend time with it. Adult cats, of course, are very familiar with the litter box and generally require less training, and they're less frisky and are less likely to damage furniture by scratching it. Well-adjusted cats also are less likely to bite members of your family.

HOW ABOUT A KITTEN? After ten weeks. The first ten weeks is a crucial time for kittens to be with their mothers, learning feline manners and socialization skills. Young kittens also need their mothers' nourishment, which helps them fight infections. A weeks-old kitten is very small and cute, but it needs the companionship of its mother more than anything else.

WHEN IS THE BEST TIME TO DECLAW YOUR CAT? When it's a kitten, between three and five months old. This is widely considered the safest time, and at this age, the recovery period is the shortest. Keep in mind that a cat's claws are its best defense against predators, so the vast majority of declawed cats should spend the vast majority of time indoors. **Second opinion:** Some cat lovers and vets say the best time to declaw a cat is never. They point out that declawing is painful, and they view it as akin to mutilation. You also can buy "caps," which you or your vet slide over your cat's nails. The caps are held in place with a special glue and need to be replaced every four to six weeks.

WHEN IS THE BEST TIME TO BEGIN POTTY TRAINING YOUR PUPPY? When it's about three weeks old. That's when it becomes mobile and when its mother stops stimulating it to do its business. The problem is most puppy breeders don't try to potty train puppies by then, and they almost never sell puppies before they're six or eight weeks old. So start as soon as you bring it home. If you start early, your puppy will find its own urine and poop disgusting and won't want to be near it, so you have a better chance of training it quickly. Because some puppies will take longer than others, you'll want to start right away.

WHEN IS THE BEST TIME TO FEED YOUR DOG? When you eat breakfast and dinner. An increasing number of veterinarians say it makes sense to feed a dog twice a day, not once. Giving a dog too much food at one time may cause diarrhea, indigestion or vomiting. Whenever you feed your dog, make sure you do it at about the same time every day. If you stick to a schedule, your dog will become conditioned to eating at that time. Dogs produce digestive juices that break down organic tissues. If the food doesn't arrive when the dog comes to expect it, he will rid themselves of the acid by vomiting. **Tips:** Feed your dog after everyone else eats. As far as your dog is concerned, whoever eats first is the top dog. While you're eating, don't give your dog any of your food. Make it wait. If you have children, let them feed your dog so that the dog will know it needs to obey them.

WHEN IS THE BEST TIME OF DAY TO RUN WITH YOUR DOG? The evening. The morning is good, too, because you don't have to worry as much about your dog overheating—a big concern given that, unlike you, it's covered from head to paw with a thick layer of hair. But the evening is better because not only is overheating less of a concern then, but the evening tends to be a more relaxed time of day, when you don't have to worry about getting to work. **Tips:** (1) Regardless of when you run with your dog, always offer it water afterward, and don't force your dog to drink. It will drink when it's ready. (2) Start slow.

Don't try to run three miles the first time. Your dog needs to get in shape to run longer distances.

WHEN IS THE BEST TIME OF DAY TO BRUSH YOUR DOG'S TEETH? The evening. In fact, try doing it after you and your dog return from a run, and it drinks water. There are two reasons for this. First, if your dog is a little tired, it's less likely to put up a fight when you're brushing its teeth. Second, a dog can't rinse after its teeth are brushed, and that's not a bad thing. The toothpaste gel is still at work when it's on your dog's teeth, so you should keep it from drinking water until at least thirty minutes after the brushing. So if it has just finished drinking water, it won't want any more for a while, allowing the gel to continue fighting germs in its mouth. **Tip:** Give your dog a treat after brushing, so it will associate brushing with eating a treat.

WHEN IS THE BEST TIME TO BRUSH YOUR CAT? When it's relaxing. This is when your cat is most likely to tolerate being brushed or want to be brushed. Nearly all cats get used to it and end up liking it, and that's a good thing because brushing has some pretty obvious benefits. It helps distribute natural oils that help reduce skin irritation, and it allows your cat to bond with you. **Tips:** Long-haired cats should be brushed daily and short-haired cats a couple of times per week. If your cat doesn't like to be brushed, start petting it first, then gently rub it and then brush it. Ask your vet which type of brush is best for your cat.

WHEN IS THE BEST TIME TO HAVE YOUR DOG SPAYED AND NEUTERED? Before it turns six months old. Male dogs that are neutered by then are less likely to become obese and aggressive, and jump fences, which puts them at risk of getting hit by cars or getting lost and mistreated by strangers. Female dogs that are spayed by then have much less chance of developing breast cancer. **Second opinion:** Some vets disagree, especially when it comes to neutering. Some say neutering large dogs before they turn two years old increases the likelihood that they'll get cancer, but there are no reliable studies that support that claim.

WHICH IS THE BEST TIME OF THE DAY AND DAY OF THE WEEK TO TAKE YOUR PET TO A VETERINARIAN? Nine a.m. Tuesday. By this time, vets are digging out from the weekend's emergency calls, which often don't get resolved until Monday. **The worst time?** Saturday. This is the day that most pet owners have time to go, so it's very crowded. It's also the day that you'll see pet owners who returned home from work on Friday afternoon and discovered something of concern but couldn't get to the vet's office right away. Some of these things that crop up over the weekend don't get resolved until Monday afternoon, making Monday another bad day to go to the vet's office. **Did you know?** The most popular breed of dog in America is the Labrador retriever, but in Los Angeles, it's the bulldog. In New York, it's the Yorkshire terrier, and in Miami and Detroit, it's the German shepherd.

WHEN IS THE BEST TIME OF DAY TO FIND A RUNAWAY DOG? During the day. Dogs are not nocturnal creatures and will look for a nighttime hiding place where they can sleep. During the day, they'll move about, looking for food or another dog for companionship. The good news is the vast majority of runaway dogs are found within two miles of where they live because they are not inclined to run in one direction for very long. They may run around a lot while they're away from home, but they tend to circle back rather than going in one direction. **Tip:** Make sure your dog wears a collar with a tag that includes his or her name and your address and phone number. Lost dogs without contact information tend to be taken to animal shelters or sometimes veterinarian offices. **Did you know?** Six out of ten households own pets, and pet owners tend to do the most to help lost pets that they find get home safely.

WHEN IS THE BEST TIME OF DAY TO FIND AND CATCH A RUNAWAY HAMSTER OR GERBIL? During the day. This is especially true for hamsters, which are nocturnal, meaning they are very active—and very hard to catch—at night. Dwarf Winter White Russian hamsters and Roborovski Dwarf hamsters, two common breeds, are quick and agile and can be especially difficult to catch. Gerbils are generally even more challenging to catch. They are active at night but are more accurately described as crepuscular animals, which are most active just before dawn and just after dusk.

WHEN IS THE BEST TIME OF DAY TO BUY A HAMSTER OR GERBIL? At night. They're more active then, and you can get a sense at that time if you'll be able to handle them and catch them when they escape. During the day, they like to sleep and are a bit lazy and, some say, boring. **Bonus question: When is the best time in a hamster's life to buy one?** When it is between four and seven weeks old. Veterinarians say they're less likely at that age to be afraid when people pick them up and stroke and pet them. Young hamsters that don't get handled are more likely to bite their owners as they age.

WHICH IS THE BEST MONTH TO HAVE YOUR DOG CHECKED FOR HEARTWORM DISEASE? April. Heartworm disease starts with a mosquito biting a dog (or a cat or a ferret) and depositing heartworm larvae, which migrate to the heart and pulmonary arteries and can grow to foot-long adults and live in the dog for five to seven years. A simple blood test can detect heartworm disease, and vets say April is the best time for that. To understand why, you need to realize that heartworm larvae infect animals only when the temperature is above 57 degrees Fahrenheit for at least two weeks straight, so dogs aren't getting infected in much of the country, including the South, between November and March. The condition can't be detected for six months, so if you have your dog tested in April and he or she tests negative, that practically eliminates the possibility that he or she was infected recently enough that the disease can't be detected. If he or she tests negative, spring is the best time to start giving your dog preventive medicine, a chewable pill that he or she receives once a month.

WHEN IS THE BEST TIME IN YOUR DOG'S LIFE TO START GIVING IT PREVENTIVE HEARTWORM MEDICINE? At six months. The companies that make this medicine would like puppies to start getting it at four weeks old, but most vets say six months is fine. That also happens to be how long it takes heartworm larvae to become adult heartworms and for a blood test to detect the disease. Some pet owners give this medicine to their dogs year-round, but most vets recommend that dogs receive it during the spring and summer, when mosquitoes are active and can transmit heartworm larvae.

WHEN IS THE BEST TIME TO GET PET INSURANCE? Skip it. The cost of pet insurance over a pet's lifetime almost always exceeds its health-care costs, according to a *Consumer Reports* analysis. The exception is if your cat or dog needs treatments and surgeries that cost many thousands of dollars. If that's the case, the insurance may save you money in the end. **Did you know?** Speaking of money, it can cost $9,400 to $14,000 to feed, groom, care for and provide veterinary care to a relatively healthy dog that lives fifteen years, according to the American Society for the Prevention of Cruelty to Animals.

IF YOU'RE GOING TO BUY PET INSURANCE ANYWAY, WHEN IS THE BEST TIME TO GET IT? When your cat or dog is young. That's because companies that sell pet insurance won't cover preexisting conditions. If your cat is a kitten and your dog is a puppy, he or she probably has no preexisting conditions, and the premiums will be lower. **Tip:** Before you buy pet insurance, make sure you know what it does and does not cover. For example, most policies do not cover routine visits and exams and hereditary conditions, such as hip dysplasia in retrievers and German shepherds. Some companies cover no illness claims whatsoever for Chinese shar-peis. And when your dog has a serious health problem, most companies don't cover 100 percent of the costs of surgeries, treatments, tests and medicine. Ninety percent is more common. **Did you know?** About seventy-five million dogs and eight-five million cats are kept as pets in the United States, and fewer than one million are insured. Americans spend nearly $15 billion a year for veterinary care. **And finally:** Here are the most common surgically removed items ingested by pets: socks, underwear, rocks, balls, chew toys, corn-cobs, bones, hair ribbons and sticks.

WHEN IS THE BEST TIME OF DAY TO RIDE A HORSE? Morning. Right after sunrise is one of the coolest times of the day, when the horse is less likely to get overheated, no matter how long you ride him or her. And in the morning, the horse is rested. If it is a popular horse that likes to be ridden, it isn't yet worn out during the morning hours.

CHAPTER FOURTEEN

AROUND THE PLAYGROUND

How often have you heard a first-time mom or dad say they wish their baby came with a how-to manual? And then those same parents want to know what they should do about the Terrible Twos and then about problems that arise after their child starts school. And it doesn't stop there. Fortunately, a lot of good doctors have shared a lot of great advice with their patients, and a lot of authors have done the same with their readers. When it comes to giving good advice about children, you can never have enough, so this chapter offers several tidbits on the best times to start teaching your child math, take your toddler on a shopping trip, put a young child in day care, teach your child to swim and more.

WHEN IS THE BEST TIME TO START GIVING COW'S MILK TO A CHILD? Children younger than one should not drink cow's milk, and children between one and two should not have reduced-fat milk. After age two, however, many pediatricians recommend children drink reduced-fat cow's milk because older children do not need as much fat in their diets. **Did you know?** Pediatricians say mothers' milk is the healthiest drink for a newborn, and they want older children to drink lots of water and milk, but doctors discourage parents from giving their children juice because it contains so much sugar.

WHEN IS THE BEST TIME TO TAKE YOUR TODDLER ON A SHOPPING TRIP? About an hour after a nap. Some kids are very sleepy right after a nap, and others are all wound up. So wait a bit to get through either stage, and then go. **Tips:** Distract your child in the store by giving him something to eat, playing catch with her with a soft toy, asking him questions and offering her a special treat if she behaves.

IF YOU HAVE TO PUT YOUR YOUNG CHILD IN DAY CARE, WHEN IS THE BEST TIME TO DO IT? One year old. Young children in day care often have better language skills by three than do children who stay at home with a parent or a nanny, according to a Norwegian study. That exposure benefits their language development more than staying at home. And the ability to effectively express themselves gives them more confidence as they start school. **The downside of day care:** Another recent study shows that children in day care suffer more ear and respiratory infections than stay-at-home kids, but that evens out after the stay-at-home kids start kindergarten and become exposed to new germs from their classmates.

WHEN IS THE BEST TIME TO START TEACHING YOUR CHILD MATH? At fourteen months. Children as young as fourteen months who are exposed to counting do better at math by the time they start school, according to a study that videotaped forty-four children ages fourteen to thirty months. The researchers kept track of the number of times the parents counted or spoke a number word to their children. Some children heard as few as 28 per week while others heard as many as 1,799. The more counting they did as toddlers and the more numbers they heard, the more likely they were to understand basic math concepts by the time they were forty-six months old. **What you can do:** Keep counting to and with your toddlers even if they don't seem to understand. Researchers say it will pay off.

WHEN IS THE BEST TIME OF DAY TO READ TO YOUR CHILD IF YOU WANT HIM OR HER TO REMEMBER IT FOR A LONG TIME? Starting at 8 p.m. At that time, our nervous system is aroused, and long-term memory improves during this time. The theory is that when our nervous systems are aroused, our brains pay closer attention to what they find important and interesting. For people who usually sleep at night and are awake during the day, fatigue sets in at about midnight, and that's when the benefits of late-night study end.

WHEN IS THE BEST TIME TO TEST A CHILD TO DETERMINE IF HE IS GIFTED? Ages four to eight. The results from achievement or intelligence tests given to children younger than four are considered unreliable because children that young may not take the test seriously and may intentionally answer questions incorrectly. Test scores for children older than eight are also often considered inaccurate for a number of reasons. Many older students feel the pressure and may underachieve.

WHEN IS THE BEST TIME TO HAVE YOUR CHILD START WRITING THANK-YOU NOTES? When he or she is old enough to write. Teach your children that in this age of e-mail and text messages people still love to receive thank-you cards. If children start writing these notes at an early age, it's more likely that it will become a lifelong habit, and it may pay off in big ways. For example, hiring managers and human resources professionals still urge job seekers who receive an interview to send handwritten notes, which are much less forgettable than e-mail messages. **Tip:** (1) Make sure your child not only thanks the gift giver but also expresses enthusiasm for the gift. (2) It's usually a good idea to help your child figure out what to write, but let him or her personally write the note, misspellings and all. It will mean more to the recipient.

WHICH IS THE BEST TIME IN YOUR CHILD'S LIFE TO START TEACHING HIM OR HER TO SWIM? One—as in one year old. Plenty of studies show that children as young as one may be less likely to drown if they take swimming lessons. Many swimming instructors say the earlier children get in the pool, the better. The American Academy of Pediatrics says parents need to decide based on how ready—physically and emotionally—their children are for lessons and on how often their children come in contact with swimming pools, lakes, rivers and other bodies of water.

WHICH IS THE BEST TIME OF YEAR TO TEACH YOUR CHILD TO RIDE A BICYCLE? Spring and summer. The weather and your surroundings—no leaves or ice to slip on—are less likely to interfere with learning. **Tip:** Teach your child to ride on a lawn, a grassy field or any place that provides a soft landing spot when they fall. Many children take longer to ride a bike because they're afraid of falling and getting hurt. Take that fear out of the equation, and they'll get right back on their bicycles and learn more quickly.

WHICH IS THE BEST TIME IN YOUR CHILD'S LIFE TO TEACH HIM OR HER TO RIDE A BICYCLE WITHOUT TRAINING WHEELS? Most six-year-olds are ready, but some can learn as early as four. How do you know if your children are ready? If they have good balance and coordination. How do you know if they have good balance and coordination? If they can hop on one foot for thirty seconds or spin around without falling. Another good way to prepare children for a bicycle without training wheels is to put them on a twelve-inch bicycle *with* training wheels. Many children who have learned how to steer a tricycle are ready for a short bike with training wheels when they're as young as two and a half years old.

WHEN IS THE BEST TIME TO HAVE A CHILD'S TONSILS REMOVED? After a child has had numerous sore throats, especially if the sore throats are caused by strep. During the 1960s and 1970s, doctors performed about one million tonsillectomies a year. In recent years, with a much larger population of children, they do about 250,000 a year. The threshold these days for tonsillectomies is if the tonsils are so swollen that it makes breathing and swallowing difficult. The surgeries tend to help reduce sore throats in the short term but have very little long-term effects.

WHEN IS THE BEST TIME TO TURN OFF THE TV FOR KIDS? After two hours. A growing number of pediatricians and nutritionists say children should watch no more than two hours of TV a day. 5210 Let's Go!, an antiobesity program in Maine, has jumped on this bandwagon. As the name implies, it urges children to eat at least five fruits or vegetables a day, watch no more than two hours of TV a day, spend at least one hour a day exercising and consume no sugary drinks, only water or low-fat milk. Officials in Maine say the program has helped reduce childhood obesity there. **Did you know?** Residents of Vermont eat the most fruits and vegetables—29.3 percent eat the recommended amount—followed by Connecticut, Maine, New Hampshire and California.

WHICH IS THE BEST AGE TO BUY YOUR CHILD A CELL PHONE FOR THE FIRST TIME? When your child is mature enough to walk to and from school alone, take the city bus and go to other neighborhoods unaccompanied. Then it might make sense for children to have a phone so they can let parents know where they are or call 9-1-1 if they are endangered. The earliest age? That's probably around nine or ten, but regardless of the age, parents must discuss the responsibilities that come with having a cell phone, and they must check to see how their child is using it. Don't just say you'll monitor the phone—actually do it. Also, don't hesitate to take it away if your child is misusing it, if his grades slip after he gets it or if he is using it late at night in his bedroom after he should be asleep. **What you can do:** Consider requiring your child to pay all or part of the monthly fees associated with having a cell phone. That may cause her to treat the phone better and take steps to keep from losing it.

WHICH IS THE BEST AGE TO HAVE YOUR CHILD FITTED WITH BRACES? While your child's mouth is growing the most and when baby teeth are gone or mostly gone. That's going to be around eleven or twelve. When a lot of growth is occurring, orthodontists can do more to guide teeth into their proper place. For girls, most growth occurs right before the teen years, and that explains why eleven, twelve and thirteen are the most common ages for girls to receive braces. Boys often are a couple of years behind. Of course, the best time also depends on the problem that needs to be corrected and how serious it is. Orthodontists sometimes will want to fix a severe cross-bite as soon as they see it, even if the child is five or six. If the problem isn't severe, they tend to wait until baby teeth are gone and a lot of growth is taking place inside a child's mouth.

WHICH IS THE BEST TIME OF DAY TO SEE YOUR ORTHODONTIST? Midmorning and early afternoon, when you are less likely to wait too long to receive treatment. Many adults want to schedule their appointments first thing in the morning before they go to work, and most parents want to schedule their children's appointments after school. Those times tend to be hectic in most orthodontist offices. **Tip:** After-school appointments can lead to the longest waits in your orthodontist's office. Find an afternoon when your child can leave school early without missing a test or anything too important and schedule an appointment then so you can beat the rush. School administrators tend to be very understanding, and your child shouldn't find it too difficult to make up the work he or she missed.

AND WHICH IS THE BEST MONTH FOR A NEW PATIENT CONSULTATION WITH AN ORTHODONTIST? May or June, or October or November. An appointment in May or June means your child can receive braces in the summer, and they'll have time to get used to them before school starts. October or November makes sense if your dental deductible has been met by then and if your insurance company pays for orthodontic work. **The worst month?** July or August. Summer is the busiest time of the year at most orthodontist offices, where children are getting their braces placed or removed before school starts. It's not always easy to get a convenient appointment then.

WHEN IS THE BEST TIME TO HAVE YOUR CHILD'S EARS PIERCED? When he or she is old enough to care for the earrings—and their earlobes—himself or herself and old enough to understand the risks of infections, allergic reactions and earrings embedded in the lobe. This is according to the American Academy of Pediatrics. Pediatricians also point out that the chance of a child swallowing earring parts goes way down after the age of four or five. **Second opinion:** Some parents recommend ear piercing the earlier the better, so your child will not remember what can be a painful and scary experience. **What you can do:** If you decide to have your baby's ears pierced, ask her doctor to do it. Some doctors would prefer you ask them to do it rather than having it done at your home or at a shopping mall store, which may not use tools that are clean and sterile.

WHEN IS THE BEST TIME TO GIVE MEDICINE TO A FEVERISH CHILD? Only when the child is experiencing some other symptom, such as pain, dehydration, rash, swollen glands, confusion, shortness of breath or seizures. The American Academy of Pediatrics recommends not giving fever-reducing medicine to a child who is otherwise comfortable. Many pediatricians agree and say fever alone rarely is cause for concern. **What you can do:** If you're concerned about your child's fever, call your doctor if the fever is between 100.4 and 103 degrees for children under six months, and if it exceeds 103 degrees for older children.

SOURCES

The vast majority of what you've just read did not include attribution, but it's the result of an incredible amount of research, which included hundreds of interviews with people who deserve to be called experts. I have listed my sources in this section. It's worth explaining why I didn't list all my sources by name. In many cases, multiple sources said the exact same thing, so I decided to save a few trees by using a general attribution, such as "numerous grocers" or "several attorneys." In other cases, I protected the identity of sources who provided little-known information that their supervisors wouldn't have wanted them to share—such as shopping tips that save consumers money but cost companies money. It's also worth noting that in a few cases, I drew best-time conclusions that my sources were unwilling or unable to make.

GETTING IT

Buy a high-definition TV–Appliance managers at Best Buy, Circuit City and Walmart
Buy things online–ShopItToMe.com, which tracks online sales from more than one hundred retailers; Farnoosh Tarobi, personal finance expert and author, "Cheapest Days to Shop Online," CBS MoneyWatch.com, August 11, 2010
Shop online for Christmas gifts–"Your Guide to the Best Times to Shop Online," *Real Simple*, November 2011
Buy a cell phone–Stephanie Sanford, care specialist, Sprint Nextel Corporation
Buy an iPad–Managers at Best Buy, Target and Walmart
Negotiate a better deal on your phone and cable service–Ramit Sethi, author, *I Will Teach You to Be Rich* (Workman Publishing Company, 2009)
Buy a gym membership and start using it–Managers at Onelife Fitness and Bally Fitness
Shop at a warehouse store–Costco; Sam's Club
Buy clothes–Marshall Cohen, analyst, The NPD Group, Inc., a consumer market research company
Buy suits–Brooks Brothers, Jos. A. Banks, Men's Warehouse salesmen
Buy fancy dresses for proms or weddings–Alan Fields, coauthor, *Bridal Bargains* (Windsor Peak Press, 2008)
Buy perfume–Fragrance department managers at Dillard's, Macy's and Nordstrom's
Buy deodorant–Grocery store managers
Buy diamonds/jewelry–Numerous jewelers
Buy Broadway tickets–Broadway theater employees
Buy a gift card–Dan Horne, a professor of marketing at Providence College, also known as the "gift card guru"; Erin Huffstetler, *Frugal Living* columnist, "Buy Gift Cards for Less," About.com

Buy Christmas cards—Managers at Target and Walmart

Buy calendars—Numerous bookstore managers

Renew a magazine subscription—Association of Magazine Media; subscription service specialists for Meredith Corporation, Condé Nast

Buy college textbooks—Numerous college students and bookstore managers

Buy backpacks—Managers at Target and Walmart

Buy tents, lanterns, sleeping bags and other camping gear—Bass Pro Shops salesmen

Upgrade your computer—Chris Pirillo, self-described geek, Internet entrepreneur, hardware addict, software junkie; Stan Miastkowski, contributing editor, "Upgrade or Buy a New PC?," *PCWorld,* January 29, 2003

Buy patio furniture—Outdoor and garden department managers at Lowe's and Home Depot

Buy a swing set—Managers at Walmart and Kmart

Buy a pool or hot tub—Pool and spa managers, including Mike DiPersio, sales professional, East Coast Leisure, Newport News, Virginia

Buy flip-flops—Managers at Walmart and Kmart; American Academy of Ophthalmology

Buy a dehumidifier—Managers at Lowe's and Home Depot

Buy carpeting and flooring—Carpet Express, Haynes store managers

Buy a mattress and box spring—Shivani Vora, lifestyle and travel writer, "How to Get a Cheaper Mattress," *Real Simple,* September 2011

Buy a timeshare—Numerous timeshare salesmen and owners

Check for new coupons—coupons.com, redplum.com, thriftytiff.com

Buy prepared foods—Numerous grocers; Shivani Vora, lifestyle and travel editor, "How to Cut Your Food Bill," *Real Simple,* November 2011

GETTING RID OF IT

Go to a garage sale—Veteran garage sale sellers and shoppers throughout the nation

Sell something at a live auction—Inchang Yang and Byungnam Kahng, mathematicians at Seoul National University, Korea, "Bidding Process in On-line Auctions and Winning Strategy: Rate Equation Approach," *Physical Review E,* June 2006; Harvard economist Alvin Roth, *American Economic Review,* 2002; Ulrike Malmendier and Young Han Lee, assistant professors of economics at University of California, Berkeley, "The Bidder's Curse," National Bureau of Economic Research working paper, December 2007

Sell household goods online—Craigslist; eBay

Post/expect hits on Craigslist—Craigslist

Sell a vacation home—Real estate agents in New York, North Carolina, New Jersey and Arizona

Sell stocks—Jayne Di Vincenzo, president, Lions Bridge Financial, Newport News, Virginia; Stock Trader's Almanac; Bespoke Investment Group; Adam Shell, reporter, "Dow Hits April on Upswing," *USA Today,* April 2, 2011; SunAmerica Capital Services, Inc.

Sell gold—Levi Family Jewelers, San Diego; Alix Steel, senior producer/markets reporter, "Gold Prices: Where Will They Finish 2011?" *The Street,* August 2, 2011

Throw out old tax returns—Numerous accountants, including Michael Mendelsohn of Dixon Hughes Goodman LLP, in Newport News, Virginia; "Do Keep Financial Documents for Tax Records," *Consumer Reports Money Adviser,* Vol. 7, Issue 6, 2011

Get rid of a credit card—"New Plastic Can Ding Your Credit Score," *Consumer Reports,* August 2011

Sell sports cards–Nick Tylwalk, sportswriter, "Best Times to Sell Sports Cards," About.com Guide

Sell NFL tickets–Longtime NFL fans throughout the nation

Throw out meat, dairy foods, canned goods and soda and dry goods–U.S. Department of Agriculture

Throw out nonprescription drugs and vitamins–U.S. Food and Drug Administration

Throw out over-the-counter medication–U.S. Food and Drug Administration; U.S. Environmental Protection Agency; American Pharmacists Association and U.S. Fish and Wildlife Service

Replace your toothbrush–American Dental Association; Centers for Disease Control and Prevention

GETTING THINGS DONE

Start a habit–Several behavioral psychologists

Go to the post office–U.S. Postal Service employees

Mail something that will be promptly read–U.S. Postal Service; Vertis Communications' Customer Focus Direct Mail Study, 2007

Read a newspaper online–Newspaper executives

Post something on Facebook–Jefferson Graham, technology reporter, "5 Tips to Make Social-Media Marketing Sing," *USA Today,* August 10, 2011

Confront someone who "unfriended" you on Facebook–Judith Newman, columnist, "Manner Up!" *Parade,* May 29, 2011

Tweet/retweet–Malcolm Coles SEO consultant and freelance content strategist from London; Dan Macsai, assistant editor, "Report: Nine Scientifically Proven Ways to Get

Retweeted on Twitter," fastcompany.com, September 21, 2009; thesocialmediaguide .com; Christopher Shea, freelance writer, "Who Tweets?,"*Wall Street Journal*, May 21–22, 2011.

Dunk your cell phone in a pot of dry rice–Chris Gaylord, staff writer, "When a Low-Tech Fix Is All You Need," *Christian Science Monitor*, March 21, 2011

Knit–Lynne Lamburg and Michael Smolensky, authors, *The Body Clock Guide to Better Health* (Henry Holt and Co., 2000)

Catch someone in a lie–Arianne Cohen and Lindsy Van Gelder, writers, "5 Ways to Tell If Someone Is Lying," *Real Simple*, July 2011

Go on a whale watching trip–*Consumer Reports*, July 2009

See stars in the night sky–Adler Planetarium, Chicago

Golf–Numerous golfers and golf course managers throughout the country

Ski or snowboard–Colorado Ski Country USA, Utah Outside, Ski NH and other groups that promote skiing and outdoor winter activities

Have a snack before you work out–"Snack FAQs," *Real Simple*, September 2011; Lisa Kovalovich, freelance writer, "11 Energy-Boosting Snacks," *Fitness Magazine*, December 2005

Bowl–Bowling alley owners throughout the country

Hunt–U.S. Fish and Wildlife Service; numerous hunters and outdoorsmen

Hunt and fish–FieldAndStream.com

Get engaged–Myreah Moore, coauthor, *Date Like a Man* (HarperPaperbacks, 2001); Match.com; Jewelers of America; The Knot Inc., a lifestyles media company

Break off an engagement–American Heart Association

Elope–The Knot, Inc., a lifestyle media company; Joshua M. Ackerman, assistant professor of marketing, et al., "Let's Get Serious: Communicating Commitment in Romantic Relationships," *Journal of Personality and Social Psychology*, June 2011

Enter a nursing home—Joseph Law, administrator, James River Convalescent Center, Newport News, Virginia; U.S. Department of Health and Human Services

Ask for a favor—Marcus Wynne, freelance writer and author, "If It's Thursday, Ask for a Raise," *Psychology Today,* September 1, 1998; Debbie Moskowitz, psychologist at McGill University, Montreal

Find volunteers—International Medical Volunteers Association

Go to a musical or other theatrical performance—Rosie Di Vincenzo, stage manager

Audition for a play—Numerous actors

Sing—Ellen Petko, voice teacher and vocal coach

Run your dishwasher or washer and dryer—*Consumer Reports,* July 2009

GETTING AROUND

Take your car in for a repair—Bundle Report; car repair shop owners

Take your vehicle to a car wash—*Consumer Reports,* July 2009

Sell a used car—National Automobile Dealers Association; U.S. Department of Commerce

Lease a car—LeaseGuide.com; Mark Solheim, senior editor, "Five Myths on Leasing a Car," *Kiplinger's Personal Finance,* February 2008; "A Few Savvy Car-Buying (or Leasing) Strategies," finweb.com

Buy an electric or hybrid car—Jeff Bartlett, deputy online automotive editor at *Consumer Reports*

Get a loan on a new car—Car dealers nationwide

Sell a used motorcycle—Several motorcycle dealers

Buy recreational vehicles—Numerous RV dealers

Drive and live to tell about it—Insurance Institute for Highway Safety

Allow teens to get a driver's license—Insurance Institute for Highway Safety

Novice driver to learn to drive on the highway—American Automobile Association; American Academy of Child and Adolescent Psychiatry

Stop seniors from driving—Insurance Institute of Highway Safety

Get into a car with an older driver—Jennifer Corbett Dooren, health reporter, Dow Jones Newswires, "Study: Kids Safer with Grandparents Driving," *Wall Street Journal,* July 19, 2011

Get the best gas mileage—U.S. Energy Department; Mike Allen, senior editor, automotive, "Fighting $4 Fuel," *Popular Mechanics,* July 2011

Change the oil in your car/rotate your tires—Several mechanics

Charge an electric car—Tammy M. Thompson, postdoctoral associate, Massachusetts Institute of Technology, et al., "Air Quality Impacts of Plug-In Hybrid Electric Vehicles in Texas: Evaluating Three Battery Charging Scenarios," *Environmental Research Letters,* May–June 2011

Buy/sell a yacht—National Marine Manufacturers Association

Buy a new kayak—Smart-Start-Kayaking

GETTING PRETTY

Get your hair done—Rachel Barbery, manager, Supercuts, Newport News, Virginia

Color your hair—Numerous hairstylists

Shave your legs—"4 Smart De-fuzzing Tricks," *Glamour,* July 2011

Shave–Jennifer Ackerman, author, *Sex Sleep Eat Drink Dream: A Day in the Life of Your Body* (Houghton Mifflin Co., 2007)

Shave off your beard–Joe Kita, author and freelance writer, "Special Father's Day Edition Health Quiz," *Parade*, June 19, 2011

Have hair removal treatments–American Society of Plastic Surgeons

Get body parts waxed–Several waxing technicians

Get a Botox injection–American Society of Plastic Surgeons

Get other cosmetic plastic surgery/breast augmentation surgery–American Society of Plastic Surgeons; SF Plastic Surgery & Laser Center

Whiten your teeth–Consumer Guide to Dentistry

Do a body piercing–" 'Tis the Season to Be Tattooed," About.com

Get a facial/nails done–Numerous salon owners; "Seasonal Pointers," *Real Simple*, November 2011

GETTING RICH

Buy stocks–Bespoke Investment Group; Adam Shell, reporter, "Dow Hits April on Upswing," *USA Today*, April 2, 2011; SunAmerica Capital Services, Inc.

Buy an immediate annuity–Anne Tergesen and Leslie Scism, reporters, "Is It Time to Buy an Annuity?" *Wall Street Journal*, May 14–15, 2011.

Buy individual life/auto insurance–Numerous insurance agents, including Nelson Kelley of AllState in Newport News, Virginia

Buy long-term care insurance–American Association for Long-Term Care Insurance

Give to charity–Bundle Report; Missouri Department of Economic Development

Ask for a donation–Richard Patrick Martin, economist, University of Regina, Saskatchewan, and John Randal, economist, Victoria University of Wellington, New Zealand, "How Sunday, Price and Serial Norms Influence Donation Behaviour," *Journal of Socio-Economics*, October 2009

Pick up the check–"6 Things Not to Worry About on a First Date," *Glamour*, July 2011

Wire money–Bob Bailey, chief executive officer, Colonial Virginia Bank, Gloucester, Virginia

Lock in your interest rate–Tony Woodward, loan officer, Southern Trust Mortgage, a division of Middleburg Bank

Borrow from your 401(k)–Jason Zweig, columnist, "Banking on Yourself: Is It Ever OK to Raid Your 401(k)?," *Wall Street Journal*, June 25–26, 2011

Pay your credit card bill–Leslie McFadden, Credit Card Adviser columnist, "When Is Best Time to Pay Credit Card?," Bankrate.com, May 13, 2009

Apply for a credit card for the first time/if you already have one–Leslie McFadden, Credit Card Adviser columnist, "Best Time to Apply for a Credit Card," Bankrate.com, March 17, 2010

Get money from an ATM if you live in a crime-ridden neighborhood–Marcus Felson, professor of criminal justice at Rutgers University, and Erika Poulsen, research director at the Crime Mapping Research Lab at the School of Criminal Justice at Rutgers University, "Simple Indicators of Crime by Time of Day," *International Journal of Forecasting*, 2003; Mint.com.

Balance your checkbook–Debby Fowles, financial planning guide, About.com

Save your loose change–American Bankers Association

Lend money to a relative or friend–Gerri Detweiler, Credit.com's personal finance expert, "The Best Ways to Loan Money to Friends and Family," Credit.com

Get an estate plan–Numerous estate-planning attorneys, including Geneva N. Perry of McDermottWard, Hampton, Virginia, and Harold H. "Bart" Barton Jr., Mulkey, Reid & Barton, Newport News, Virginia

Write a will–Numerous estate-planning attorneys, including Geneva N. Perry of McDermottWard, Hampton, Virginia, and Harold H. "Bart" Barton Jr., Mulkey, Reid & Barton, Newport News, Virginia

Put the brakes on excessive spending habits–Jayne Di Vincenzo, president, Lions Bridge Financial, Newport News, Virginia

File for bankruptcy–Several bankruptcy attorneys, including Virginia attorney Linda W. Coppinger

Move your money to an out-of-state bank account–Kimberly Thorpe, freelance writer, "Take This APR and Shove It," *Mother Jones,* January/February 2011

GETTING HEALTHY

Go to the doctor and expect to get in and out quickly–Numerous doctors

Admitted to a hospital if you don't want to stay long–Institute for Public Policy Research

Receive anesthesia–Melanie C. Wright, assistant professor of anesthesiology and director of research at the Duke Human Simulation and Patient Safety Center at Duke University Medical Center, et al., "Time of Day Effects on the Incidence of Anesthetic Adverse Events," *Quality & Safety in Health Care,* August 2006, National Institutes of Health

See a nutritionist–American Dietetic Association

Have your hearing checked–National Center for Hearing Assessment and Management; American Academy of Pediatrics

Have your eyes examined–American Optometric Association

Use those machines that promise to stimulate muscle growth–U.S. Food and Drug Administration

Lose weight–Meryl Davids Landau, freelance writer, "5 Things You Didn't Know About . . . Weight Loss," *Parade*, April 17, 2011; Gina Kolata, science writer, "Calorie-Burning Fat? Studies Say You Have It," April 8, 2009, *New York Times*

Exercise if you're trying to lose weight–America's Health Rankings

Stretch your muscles to avoid cramping during exercise–Alex Hutchinson, contributing editor, "Stretching Prepares Your Body for Exercise," *Popular Mechanics,* September 2011

Check a resting heart rate–*New York Times* Health Guide

Be asleep–Numerous doctors

Take your temperature–Centers for Disease Control and Prevention

Drink alcohol if you're trying to avoid a hangover–Damaris Rohsenow, professor of community health, Brown University, et al., "Intoxication with Bourbon Versus Vodka: Effects on Hangover, Sleep, and Next-Day Neurocognitive Performance in Young Adults," *Alcoholism: Clinical and Experimental Research,* December 2009

Get a massage–Numerous masseuses

Get a massage if you're having your period–American Massage Therapy Association

Expose yourself to the sun–M. Nathaniel Mead, nutrition educator, consultant, writer, "Benefits of Sunlight: A Bright Spot for Human Health," *Environmental Health Perspectives,* April 2008

Expose yourself to the sun in the hopes of getting the most vitamin D–Johan Moan, professor, Department of Radiation Biology, Institute for Cancer Research, Montebello, Oslo, Norway, "At What Time Should One Go Out in the Sun?," *Advances in Experimental Medicine and Biology,* 2008; National Cancer Institute at the National Institutes of Health

Tan–Prue Salasky, reporter, " 'There Is No Such Thing as a Healthy Tan,' Expert Says," *Daily Press,* April 23, 2011

Throw out an old bottle of sunscreen–American Academy of Dermatology

Diabetic to stay indoors–Prue Salasky and Veronica Chufo, health columnists, "Follow These Tips to Better Manage Diabetes in Summer," *Daily Press,* July 13, 2011

Check your moles–Alison Johnson, freelance writer, "How to Check Your Skin for Dangerous Moles," Tribune Newspapers, June 18, 2011

Get checked out by a dermatologist–American Academy of Dermatology

Take vitamin supplements and medicine–National Institutes of Health

Women to take fish-oil pills–Alice Park, staff writer, "Babies First Pill?," *Time,* August 15, 2011; March of Dimes

Take thyroid medication–U.S. Food and Drug Administration

Take calcium–National Institutes of Health; Katherine Zeratsky, Mayo Clinic nutritionist; National Academy of Sciences

Take bone-building drugs–U.S. Food and Drug Administration

Take a bone-density test–Mayo Clinic

Take a fiber supplement–U.S. Food and Drug Administration

Take blood pressure medicine–American Heart Association; "What Time You Take Blood Pressure Pills Matters," Associated Press, December 17, 2007

Take antidepressants–U.S. Food and Drug Administration

Take silver supplements–U.S. Food and Drug Administration; National Institutes of Health National Center for Complementary and Alternative Medicine

Receive the meningitis vaccine–Centers for Disease Control and Prevention

Undergo a colonoscopy–Suryakanth R. Gurudu, gastroenterologist, Mayo Clinic Arizona, et al., "Adenoma Detection Rate Is Not Influenced by the Timing of Colonoscopy When Performed in Half-Day Blocks," *American Journal of Gastroenterology,* April 19, 2011

Get checked for prostate cancer–American Urological Association

Take Viagra–Pfizer

Seek male infertility treatment–Eastern Virginia Medical School Jones Institute for Reproductive Medicine

Female infertility treatment–National Women's Health Information Center, U.S. Department of Health and Human Services

Use a cotton swab to clean the wax out of your ears–American Academy of Otolaryngology

Remove extended-wear contact lenses–American Optometric Association

Start using decongestants–*Consumer Reports,* January 2007

Get a flu shot–Mayo Clinic; Centers for Disease Control and Prevention

Get rid of cold sores–Mayo Clinic; Bryan Cullen, professor of molecular genetics and microbiology at Duke University, et al., "MicroRNAs Expressed by Herpes Simplex Virus 1 During Latent Infection Regulate Viral mRNAs," *Nature,* July 2008; National Institutes of Health

Conceive–National Institutes of Health

Receive a pelvic exam–National Cancer Institute; U.S. Department of Health and Human Services Office on Women's Health

Get the HPV vaccine–Centers for Disease Control and Prevention

Take a girl to her first appointment with a gynecologist–Heidi Stevens, freelance writer, "Timing a Girl's First Visit," Tribune Newspapers, April 23, 2011; American College of Obstetricians and Gynecologists

Do a breast exam on yourself–American Cancer Society, American College of OB/GYN,

American College of Radiology, American Society of Breast Disease, American College of Surgeons and the Society for Breast Imaging

Get a mammogram–American Cancer Society, American College of OB/GYN, American College of Radiology, American Society of Breast Disease, American College of Surgeons and the Society for Breast Imaging

Get a root canal or undergo some other sort of painful procedure–Rebecca Booth, author, *The Venus Week* (Da Capo Press, 2008)

Get a hysteroscopy–National Institutes of Health

Perform a circumcision–National Institutes of Health; American Academy of Pediatrics; American Medical Association

Eat to help strengthen your teeth–National Oral Health Information Clearinghouse; National Women's Health Resource Center

Go to the dentist–Maria Clarinda A. Buencamino, et al., "How Menopause Affects Oral Health, and What We Can Do About It," *Cleveland Clinic Journal of Medicine*, August 2009

Floss–America's Health Rankings

Get braces for adults–Vicki Ross, orthodontist, Newport News, Virginia; American Association of Orthodontists

Eat salmon, strawberries, whole-grain bread and pistachios–Nancy Kalish, freelance health journalist, "Surprising Secrets to a Great Smile," *Parade*, July 24, 2011

Get a second opinion–American Medical Association

Apply for Medicare–Earl Johnson Sr., public relations officer, Social Security Administration

GETTING THE JOB DONE

Interview for a job–Several hiring managers

Get something accomplished–Accountemps, a worldwide staffing agency

Read reports–Thomas Friberg, chief of retina services at the University of Pittsburgh Medical Center, netscape.com

Ask for a promotion–LinkedIn Corp.; Dave Baldwin, freelance writer, "Best Time to Ask for a Promotion," *Real Simple,* July 2011: OfficeTeam, a California-based staffing services company

Start work and expect less fatigue in the workplace–Associated Professional Sleep Societies, an Illinois-based joint venture of the American Academy of Sleep Medicine and the Sleep Research Society

Find a headhunter to help you find a job–Lei Han, career coach, "When and How to Use a Headhunter," bemycareercoach.com, June 24, 2011

Announce your retirement–Janet Kidd Stewart, freelance columnist, "Timing of Notice Can Carry Unwanted Effects," *Chicago Tribune,* July 3, 2011

Expect good attendance at a meeting–Kronos, Belgian-based workforce management company that advises other companies on managing absenteeism, among other things

Hold a meeting to expect the best attendance–Business owners and managers

Hire talented workers–Numerous recruiters and headhunters

Call your financial adviser–Jayne Di Vincenzo, president, Lions Bridge Financial, Newport News, Virginia

Call a criminal defense lawyer–Numerous defense attorneys

Call your lawyer and expect a quick callback–Numerous attorneys, including Michael B. Ware, lawyer, Newport News, Virginia

Buy office furniture and equipment—Office Max and Office Depot furniture department managers

Hire computer geeks not associated with your computer's manufacturer—*Consumer Reports,* June 2007

Schedule an out-of-town conference, training program or board meeting—Heather Martin, director of global accounts, Helms Briscoe, a meeting scheduling firm

Contact debtors—David P. Montana, business adviser and debt collection expert

Pay bills—Barbara Haslip, freelance writer, "Cost-Cutting Ideas You Might Not Have Thought Of," *Wall Street Journal,* May 16, 2011

Buy or lease commercial real estate—Numerous real estate brokers, including Tom Waltz, principal broker, Campana Waltz Commercial Real Estate, Newport News, Virginia

Review the investment company that administers your 401(k)—Jayne Di Vincenzo, president, Lions Bridge Financial, a 401(k) plan advisory firm, Newport News, Virginia

AROUND THE HOUSE

Have a new roof put on your house and save a lot of money—Numerous roofers

Have a new roof put on your house and expect the best job—Numerous roofers, including Jim Hicks, owner of Jim Hicks Enterprises, a roofing and home remodeling company

Clean your gutters—GuttersToShutters.com

Clean your garage—Meredith Bryan, staff writer, "Peter Walsh's Life-Changing Garage Makeover," *O, The Oprah Magazine,* February 8, 2011

Hire a good housekeeper—Several sought-after housekeepers

Wash windows—"How to Get Rid of Window Streaks," HowToGetRidOfStuff.com, November 24, 2008

Vacuum–Michael Smolensky, coauthor of *The Body Clock Guide to Better Health* (Henry Holt and Co., 2000)

Have carpets professionally cleaned–Numerous carpet cleaning companies, including Stanley Steemer

Hire a painter–Numerous painters, including Robert Trent, owner, Poquoson Painting, Poquoson, Virginia

Have your house appraised–Several appraisers, including Jay Hatten of Hatten Appraisal Services, Newport News, Virginia

Sign an apartment lease–Apartment managers in Virginia, California and New York

Get the attention of your home loan officer–Mortgage loan officers, including Tony Woodward of Southern Trust Mortgage, a division of Middleburg Bank

Close on a mortgage–Mortgage loan officers, including Tony Woodward of Southern Trust Mortgage, a division of Middleburg Bank

Sign a contract to have a new house built–National Association of Home Builders; numerous contractors

Replace your air-conditioning system/heat pump–Several HVAC contractors

Replace your water heater–Numerous plumbers, including Pete's Plumbing, Inc., of Alpharetta, Georgia

Replace a wax ring on a commode–Mike McClintock, reporter, Tribune Newspapers, "When, How to Replace Wax Ring on Commode," *Daily Press*, March 17, 2011

AROUND THE WORLD

Book a hotel room–Sales reps at Wyndham Worldwide, Marriott International and Hilton Corp.; Myle Ott, computer science PhD student, Cornell University, et al., "Finding

Deceptive Opinion Spam by Any Stretch of the Imagination," independent study, 2011

Get the attention of a hotel concierge—"How to Get a Free Hotel Room Upgrade . . . From an Anonymous Concierge," *Real Simple,* June 2011

Drive cross-country—Andy Isaacson, freelance writer and photojournalist, "Riding the Rails," *New York Times,* March 5, 2009

Use frequent-flier airline miles?—IdeaWorks, a consulting firm; InsideFlyer.com

Buy travel insurance—Scott McCartney, reporter, "Coverage for When the Vacation Is Scrubbed," *Wall Street Journal,* May 19, 2011

Get a great deal on spa treatments—CruiseMates.com

Wake up in the days before traveling from the United States to Europe—Jeremy Campbell, author, *Winston Churchill's Afternoon Nap* (Simon & Schuster, 1987)

Go to the top of the Sears Tower—Willis Tower Skydeck cashiers; Willis Group Holdings

Visit New York City on a budget—Numerous travel agents and New Yorkers

Visit Hawaii—Several travel agents; National Oceanic and Atmospheric Administration

Visit Juneau, Alaska—Betsy Malloy, freelance travel writer, "Juneau, Alaska," About.com

Ski in Colorado—Travel agents; Lisa Mercer, freelance writer and author, "Best Time to Ski in Breckenridge," Demand Media

Hang glide off the dunes in Kitty Hawk—Dozens of Outer Banks residents; Outer Banks Chamber of Commerce

Scuba dive in the Caribbean—Undercurrent.org; National Association of Underwater Instructors; Professional Association of Diving Instructors

Visit Virginia Beach—Several local residents, including the author, who has lived just north of the city for twenty-six years

Visit Washington, D.C.—Longtime D.C. residents, including Mark Davidson

See the Supreme Court hear a case—www.supremecourt.gov

Visit Mexico City–Numerous travel agents and Mexico City residents

Visit the Amazon rain forest–brazil-travel-guide.com

Visit Beijing–Frommer's; Beijing resident Li Anni; Beijing native Jiao Jin

Visit New Zealand–Frommer's

Visit the Galapagos Islands–Frommer's

Take a cruise-ship vacation in Europe–Linda Garrison, About.com cruise ship guide

Visit Zanzibar–Frommer's

Visit Cape Town–Frommer's

See Victoria Falls–Frommer's

Go to Antarctica–Adventure Life travel agency; Audley Travel

Let your Facebook friends know about your vacation–"Online Exposure: Social Networks, Mobile Phones and Scams Can Threaten your Security," *Consumer Reports,* June 2011

AROUND THE KITCHEN

Cook raw vegetables–U.S. Department of Agriculture

Eat lunch–Pamela Peeke, author, *Fit to Live: The 5-Point Plan to Become Lean, Strong and Fearless for Life* (Rodale Books, 2007)

Eat a doughnut–American Dietetic Association; Nanci Hellmich, nutrition and fitness reporter, "Stay Fuller Longer with Protein, Fiber," *USA Today,* August 10, 2011; "The Case for Breakfast," *Parade,* August 21, 2011

Eat the biggest meal of the day–Helpguide.org, a free online resource that offers health advice

Eat spicy food–"Feel the Sizzle," *Daily Press,* July 13, 2011

Buy bread–Grocers and dollar-store managers

Buy disposable plates, cups and plastic forks and spoons—Numerous grocers

Start eating at a dinner party—Judith Newman, columnist, "Manner Up!," *Parade,* July 3, 2011

Start cooking after firing up a gas grill—*Consumer Reports,* June 2007; Organisation for Economic Co-operation and Development, a Paris-based group of thirty-four nations that promotes policies to improve the economic and social well-being of people around the world

Cook/season steak—"Steakology 101," *Real Simple,* September 2011

Cut steak after you take it off the grill—Steven Raichlen, author, *The Barbecue! Bible* (Workman Publishing Company, 2008)

Brush barbecue sauce on chicken— Steven Raichlen, author, *The Barbecue! Bible* (Workman Publishing Company, 2008); Harry Sawyers, associate editor, "Backyard Boardwalk," *Popular Mechanics,* September 2011

Cook chicken after defrosting it—U.S. Department of Agriculture; *Consumer Reports,* January 2007.

Uncork a bottle of wine after you buy it—John Bonne, wine columnist, "When to Open That Bottle," msnbc.com, January 27, 2005

Start drinking wine—Stacy Slinkard, wine guide and certified sommelier, "Tips for Letting Your Wine Breathe," About.com

AROUND THE YARD

Buy bushes and trees/plant flowers and plants—Managers at nursery and gardening centers

Buy garden tools—Managers at nursery and gardening centers

Mow the lawn—Numerous landscapers

Tune up your lawn mower—Roy Berendsohn, senior editor, home, "Midsummer Mower Malaise," *Popular Mechanics,* July 2011

Weed and feed your lawn—The Scotts Company

Apply weed killer—Heidi Braley, Maryland-based gardening writer

Spread mulch?—Horticulture Department, North Carolina State University

Have your soil tested—Natural Resources Conservation Service; University of Connecticut College of Agriculture and Natural Resources

Plant annuals—Landscapers in Maryland, North Carolina and Virginia

Plant bulbs—Association of Specialty Cut Flower Growers; American Flower Industry Association

Plant azaleas—United States National Arboretum

Plant pine saplings—Minnesota Department of Natural Resources

Cut down a tree that you want to use for firewood—Oregon Department of Agriculture

Prune most trees—University of Minnesota Extension Agency; Marie Iannotti, gardening guide, "Flowering Trees and Shrubs: When Is the Best Time to Prune?," About.com; Emily Green, garden writer, "The Dry Garden: Best Time to Prune Trees? Not Now," *Los Angeles Times,* April 29, 2011

Prune fruit trees—U.S. Department of Agriculture

Pick strawberries—North Carolina State University Horticulture Department

Spray for adult mosquitoes—Aatekah Mir, contributor, "Attack of the Urban Mosquitoes," *Wall Street Journal,* July 20, 2011; Illinois Department of Public Health

AROUND THE KENNEL

Buy a dog or cat–American Society for the Prevention of Cruelty to Animals; International Cat Association; American Cat Fanciers Association

Buy a kitten– International Cat Association; American Cat Fanciers Association

Declaw your cat–Numerous veterinarians

Potty training your puppy–American Kennel Club

Feed your dog–Numerous veterinarians

Run with your dog–Numerous veterinarians

Brush your dog's teeth–Numerous veterinarians

Brush your cat–Numerous veterinarians

Have your dog spayed and neutered–American Society for the Prevention of Cruelty to Animals; numerous veterinarians

Take your pet to a veterinarian–American Kennel Club; numerous veterinarians

Find a runaway dog–American Society for the Prevention of Cruelty to Animals

Buy/find and catch a hamster or gerbil–Several pet store managers

Have your dog checked for heartworm disease–Westside Animal Hospital, Fort Wayne, Indiana

Start giving it preventive heartworm medicine–Numerous veterinarians in numerous states

Buy pet insurance–"Tame Your Pet Costs," *Consumer Reports*, August 2011; American Society for the Prevention of Cruelty to Animals; American Pet Products Association; American Veterinary Medical Association; National Commission on Veterinary Economic Issues; Veterinary Pet Insurance

Ride a horse–U.S. Equestrian Federation

AROUND THE PLAYGROUND

Start giving cow's milk to a child–American Academy of Pediatrics

Take your toddler on a shopping trip–Numerous mothers in numerous states

Put your child in day care–Ratib Lekhal, researcher, Norwegian Institute of Public Health, et al., "Does Universally Accessible Child Care Protect Children from Late Talking. Results from a Norwegian Population-based Prospective," *Early Child Development and Care,* October 7, 2010; Sylvanna M. Cote, psychologist, University of Montreal, et al., "Short- and Long-Term Risk of Infections as a Function of Group Child-Care Attendance," *Archives of Pediatric and Adolescent Medicine,* December 2010

Start teaching your child math–Susan Levine, professor of psychology, University of Chicago, et al., "What Counts in the Development of Young Children's Number Knowledge," *Developmental Psychology,* November 2010

Read to your child–Jeremy Campbell, author, *Winston Churchill's Afternoon Nap* (Simon & Schuster, 1987); Michael Smolensky, professor of environmental physiology at the University of Texas School of Public Health at Houston and author of *The Body Clock Guide to Better Health* (Holt Paperbacks, 2001); Robert Strickgold, neurophysiologist, Harvard University

Test a child to determine giftedness–Carol Bainbridge, board member of the Indiana Association for the Gifted

Teach your child to swim–American Academy of Pediatrics

Teach your child to ride a bike–Sheldon "Two Wheeler" Brown, who writes about bicycles and cycling

Have a child's tonsils removed–Mayo Clinic

Turn off the TV–America's Health Rankings, an annual comprehensive assessment of the nation's health, published by United Health Foundation, the American Public Health Association and Partnership for Prevention.

Buy your child a cell phone–Kim Hart, staff writer, "From Three Dads, A Kid-Oriented Cell Phone Service," *Washington Post,* April 2, 2007

Have your child fitted with braces–Several orthodontists, including Vicki Ross, Newport News, Virginia; American Association of Orthodontists

See your orthodontist–Several orthodontists, including Vicki Ross, Newport News, Virginia; American Association of Orthodontists

Have your child's ears pierced–American Academy of Pediatrics

Give medicine to a feverish child–American Academy of Pediatrics

INDEX

Air Berlin, 135

Air Canada, 135

air conditioning, when to replace system, 128

AirTran, 136

alcohol, best way to avoid a hangover, 89

Amazon rain forest, when to visit, 141–42

American Academy of Pediatrics, 86, 101, 180, 184

American Cancer Society, 100

American College of Obstetricians and Gynecologists, 100

American Dental Association, 28

American Medical Association, 101

American Society for the Prevention of Cruelty to Animals, 173

Amtrak, 135

anesthesia, best time to receive, 85

annuals, best month to plant, 160

Antarctica, when to visit, 145

antidepressants, best time to take, 95

annuity, when to buy, 70

apartment, when to sign a lease, 126

appraisal
   best time for high, 126
   best time for low, 126
audition for a play, best time of day to, 42
azaleas, when to plant, 161

backpacks, best time to buy, 12
bankruptcy, when to file for, 78–79
Beijing, when to visit, 142
belts, when to buy online, 4
bicycle, when to teach your child to ride,
      180–81
bills, best time for a business to pay, 116
BillShrink.com, 6
blood pressure medicine, when to take, 94–95
body piercing, best time to do, 63–64
bone-building drugs, when to take, 94
bone-density test, when to get one, 94
Botox injection, when to get one, 62
bowling, best time to go, 37
braces
   best age to get, 182
   best time for adult to get, 102–103
bread, best time to buy, 151
breast augmentation, best time to get, 63
breast exam, best time to do, 100

Broadway tickets, when to buy, 9–10
Brown University, 89
bushes, when to buy, 157–58

Cabo San Lucas, when to visit, 141
calcium, best time to consume, 93–94
calendars, best time to buy, 10
camping gear, best time to buy, 12
canned goods, when to discard, 27
Cape Town, best time to visit, 144
car
   change oil, best time to, 54
   charge electric car, best time of day to, 54
   electric/hybrid, best time to buy, 50
   insurance, best time to buy, 70–71
   lease, best month to, 49
   loan, best time to get, 50
   repair, best time of week to, 48
   rotate tires, best time to, 54
   sell used car, best time to, 48–49
   wash, best time of day, 48
carpeting
   buy, best month to, 14
   have cleaned, when to, 124–25
cat
   brush, best time to, 170

cat *(continued)*
    buy, best time of year to, 168
    declaw, best time to, 168
cell phone
    buy for a child, best age to, 181–82
    dunk in rice, when to, 35
    buy, best month to, 5
    use, best time to, 35
Centers for Disease Control and Prevention, 99
charity, best month to give to, 71–72
check, when to pick up, 72
checkbook, best time to balance, 75–76
chicken
    brush with sauce, best time to, 153
    cook after defrosting, best time to, 153
children's clothes, best day to buy online, 4
Children's Hospital of Philadelphia, 53
Christmas cards, best month to buy, 10
Christmas shopping, when to shop online, 4–5
clothes, best month to buy, 7
cold sores, best time to get rid of, 98–99
colonoscopy, best time of day to get one, 96
commercial real estate, best time to buy or
    lease, 116
computer, best time to upgrade,12–13
computer geeks, best time to hire, 114–115

Con Edison, 43
conceive, when to, 99
Consumer Reports Nursing Home Guide, 41
contact lenses, best time of day to remove,
    97–98
cook
    gas grill, best time to cook with, 152
    vegetables, best time to cook, 49–50
Cornell University, 134
coupons, best month to find new ones, 15
Craigslist
    post, best day to, 22
    sell business items, best time of day to, 22
    sell personal items, best time of day to, 22
credit card
    apply for the first time, best time to, 74
    apply if have one, best time to, 75
    discard, best time to, 25
    pay bill, best time to, 73–74
criminal defense lawyer, best time of day to
    call, 113–14
cruises
    on-board deals, best time for, 136
    Europe, when to go, 143–44

dairy foods, when to discard, 26–27

deodorant, best month to buy, 8

day care, best time in child's life for, 178

Debtorboards.com, 79

debtors, best time to contact them, 115–16

decongestants, when to start using, 98

deer, best month to hunt, 38

dehumidifier, best month to buy, 14

Delta Airlines, 135

dentist, best time for women to go, 102

dental work, when to get second opinion, 103

dermatologist, best time to get checked by, 91–92

diamonds

  best price, best month to get, 8

  best selection, best month to get, 8

dinner party, best time to start eating at, 152

dishwasher, best time to run it, 42–43

disposable plates, best month to buy, 151

doctor

  go, best month to, 84

  speedy service, best day for, 84

dog

  brush teeth, best time of day to, 170

  buy, best time of year to, 168

  check for heartworms, best month to, 172–73

  feed, best time to, 169

  find runaway, best time of day to, 171

  run with, best time of day to, 169–70

  spay/neuter, best time to, 170–71

donation, best day of the week to ask for one, 72

doughnut, best time of the day to eat, 150

dresses, best time of the year to buy fancy ones, 7

drive

  cross country, best month to go, 135

  gas mileage, best time for good, 53–54

  learn to on the highway, best time of day to, 52

  safely, best time of day, 51

  teen driver's license, when to allow, 52

drugs, when to discard, 27

dry goods, when to discard, 27

ears, when to remove wax, 97

eat

  spicy food, best time to eat, 151

  biggest meal, worst time to eat, 151

Eliot, George, 167

elope, best time to, 39–40

Emirates, 135

Empire State Building, 137

engagement

    best time to end, 39

    best month to do, 39

    best time to do, 38–39

estate plan, best time to get one, 76–77

exercise, best time of the year to lose weight, 87

eye, best time to have examined, 86

Facebook

    confront someone on, best time to, 33–34

    post something, best time of day to, 33

    post vacation photos, best time to, 145–46

facial, best time of day and month to get one, 64

favor, best day of the week to ask a co-worker, 109

female infertility treatment, best time to take, 97

fiber supplement, best time to take, 94

financial adviser, best day to call, 113

fish oil, best time to take, 92–93

flip-flops, best month to buy, 14

flooring, best month to buy, 14

floss, best time of day to, 102

flowers

    buy, best month to, 158

    plant bulbs, best days of the year to, 160–61

flu shot, best time to take, 98

fly, best time to use frequent-flier miles, 135

401(k)

    borrow from, best time to, 73

    move, best month to, 117

    review, best time to, 116–17

Galapagos Islands, when to visit, 143

garage, best time of the year to clean, 123

garage sale

    best day for, 20

    best month for, 20

    best time of month for, 20

    best time of day for, 21

garden tools, best time to buy, 158

gas mileage

    best time to maximize, 53–54

gift cards, best month to buy, 10

gifted education, best time to test child, 179

gold, best time to sell, 24

golf, best day of the week, 36

gums, best time to eat certain foods to have
    healthy, 103
gutters, best month to clean, 122
gym membership, best time of year to
    buy, 6
gynecologist, best time to take a girl for the
    first time, 100

habit, best time of day to start new, 31–32
hair
    color, best time to, 60
    get done, best day of the week, 60
    removal treatments, best time to have, 61
hamster
    buy, best time to, 172
    catch, best time of the day to, 172
hang glide, best month at North Carolina's
    Outer Banks, 139
Hawaii, best month to go, 138
headhunter, best time to contact, 111
hearing, best time to have it checked, 85–86
heart rate, best time of day to check, 88
heat pump, best time to replace, 128
high-definition TVs, best month to buy, 4
hire, best time to hire talented workers,
    113

home loan officer, best time of the month to
    get attention, 126
horse, best time of day to ride, 174
hospital, best day of the week to be admitted
    for a short stay, 84
hot tub, best month to buy, 13
hotel
    book a room, best time of the year to, 134
    concierge, best time of day to attract, 134–35
house, best month to sign a contract, 127–28
household goods
    best day of the week and month to sell
        online, 21–22
housekeeper, best month to hire, 123
HPV vaccine, best time to get, 99–100
hunt
    best day of the month to, 38
    best month for deer, 38
    best time of day to, 37–38
hysteroscopy, best time to get, 101

insurance
    life, best time to buy, 70
    long-term care, best time to buy, 71
    pet, best time to buy, 173
Insurance Institute for Highway Safety, 53

INDEX

interest rate, best time of the month to lock in, 73

interview
  best order in which to, 108
  best time of day, 108
iPad, best time to buy, 5

jackets, best day of the week to buy online, 4
Japanese Golden Week, 138
JetBlue, 135
jewelry
  best time of day to buy, 9
  buy online, best day of the week to, 4
Juneau, Alaska, when to visit, 138

Katz, Steven, 79
kayak, best month to buy, 55
kitten, best time to buy, 168
knit, best time of day to, 35

lawn
  mow, best time of the day to, 158
  tune up mower, best time to, 158–59
lawyer, best time of day to expect a quick call, 114
lie, when to catch someone, 35

lingerie, best day of the week to buy online, 4
lipstick, best time for a bride to apply, 65
live auction, best time to sell at, 21
loan, best time to get for a new car, 50
Lufthansa, 135
lunch, best time of the day to eat, 150

magazine subscriptions, best time to renew, 11
mail, best day of the week to send, 32
male infertility treatment, best time to seek, 96–97
mammogram, best time to get one, 101
Massachusetts Institute of Technology, 40
massage, best time of day and time of the month to get, 89
math, best time to start teaching, 178–79
mattress, best time of the year to buy, 14–15
meat, best time to discard, 26
Medicare, best time to apply, 103
medicine, best time to give to feverish child, 183–84
meeting, best day and time of day for best attendance, 112–13
meningitis vaccine, best time to take, 95–96
men's apparel, best day of the week to buy online, 4

Mexico City, 141

milk, best time to give to child, 178

Millman, Dan, 107

moles
    best time to check, 91

money
    ATM, 75
    bankruptcy, best time to file for, 78–79
    lend to relative, best time to, 76
    save loose change, best time to, 76
    stop excessive spending, best time to, 78
    wire, best time of day to, 72–73

mortgage
    close, best time of the month to, 127
    refinance, best time to, 127

mosquitoes, best time of the day to spray for, 163

motorcycle, best month to sell, 50–51

move out of state, best month to, 127

mulch, best time of the year to spread, 159–60

muscle growth machines, best time to use, 86

muscles, best time to stretch to avoid cramping, 87

nails, best time of day and year to get done, 64–65

National Cancer Institute, 90

National Football League tickets, best month to sell, 26

New York City, best month to visit on a budget, 137–138

New Zealand, best month to go, 142–143

newspaper, best time of day to read online, 32–33

nursery, best time to paint, 125

nursing home, best month to enter, 40–41

nutritionist, best time to go, 85

office furniture, best month to buy, 114

orthodontist
    best month to go, 183
    best time of day to go, 182–83

outdoors, best time to hire painter for, 125

out-of-town conference, best days of the week and months to schedule, 115

pants, best day of the week to buy online, 4

patio furniture, best time to buy, 13

pelvic exam, best time for, 99

perfume, best month to buy, 8

pet insurance, best time to buy, 173

phone and cable service, best time to
negotiate, 6
pierce ears, best time to, 183
pine saplings, best time of the year to plant, 161
plastic surgery, best time to get, 62–63
pool, best month to buy, 13
post office, best day of the week to go to, 32
prepared foods, best time of the day to buy, 15
promotion, best month to ask for, 109
prostate cancer, best time to get checked for, 96
puppy, best time to potty train, 169

read
start teaching child to, best time of day, 179
recreational vehicles, best time of the year to
buy, 51
reports, best time of day to read, 109
retirement, best time to announce, 111–12
roof replacement
best results, best time of the year to get, 122
save money, best month to, 122
root canal, best time to get, 101

scarves, best day of the week to buy online, 4
scuba dive
in Caribbean, best month to, 139–40

Sears Tower, best time of the day to go, 137
seniors
join driving, best time to, 53
stop driving, best time to, 52–53
shave
beard, best time of the year to, 61
legs, best time to, 60
best time of day to, 60–61
shoes, best day of the week to buy online,
4
ShopItToMe.com, 4
shopping, best time to take a toddler, 178
silver supplements, best time to take, 95
sing, best time of day, 42
Singapore Airlines, 135
ski
in Colorado, best month to, 138–39
learn, best month to, 36–37
sleep, best time of the day to, 88
snowboard, best month to learn, 36–37
soil, best time of the year to test, 160
Southwest Airlines, 135
sports cards, best time to sell, 25–26
stargaze, best time to, 36
steak
cook, best time to, 152

steak (*continued*)

   cut, best time to, 153

stocks

   buy, best month to, 70

   sell, best month to, 23–24

   sell, best time to, 23

strawberries, best time of day to pick, 162–63

suits, best month to buy, 7

sun

   expose yourself, best time of day, 90

   tan, best time to, 90

   vitamin D, best time of day to get, 90

sunglasses, best time to buy, 14

sunscreen, best time to discard, 91

Supreme Court, best month to hear a case, 140–41

swim, best time to start teaching a child, 180

swimsuits, best day of the week to buy online, 4

swing set, best month to buy, 13

tan, best time to, 90

tax returns, best time to discard, 24–25

teeth

   braces, best time for adults to get, 102–03

floss, best time of the day to, 102

strengthen, best time to, 101–02

whiten, best time to, 63

temperature, best time of day to take, 88

textbooks

   electronic, best time to buy, 11–12

   print, best time to buy, 11

thank-you notes, best time to start writing them, 179–80

theater

   audition for, best time to, 42

   go, best time to, 41

thyroid medication, best time to take, 93

timeshare, best time to buy, 15

toddler, best time to take shopping, 178

toilet, best time to replace wax ring, 129

tonsils, best time to remove, 181

toothbrushes, best time to discard, 28

travel insurance, best time to buy, 136

trees

   buy, best time to, 157–158

   cut down, best time to, 161–62

   prune, best time of the year to, 162

TVs

   buy, best month to, 4

   turn off, best time to, 181

INDEX

tweet
   best day to retweet, 35
   best day of the week to, 34
   best time of day to be retweeted, 34
   best time of day, 34

US Airways, 135

vacation home, best time of year to sell, 23
vacuum, best time of day, 124
vegetables, when to cook them, 149–50
veterinarian, best time of day and day of the
   week to go, 171
Viagra, best time to take, 96
Victoria Falls, best time to see, 145
Virgin Australia, 135
Virginia Beach, best month to go, 140
vitamins
   discard, best time to, 27
   take, best time of day to, 92
volunteers, best time of the year to find,
   41

warehouse store shopping, best time of day
   and day of the week for, 6
washer/dryer, best time to run, 42–43

Washington, D.C., best time of the year to go,
   140
water heater, best time of the year to replace,
   128
wax, best time for body wax, 61–62
weed killer
   best month to apply, 159
   best time of day to apply, 159
weight, best time of the year to lose, 86–87
whale watching, best time of day to go, 36
will, best time to write, 77–78
Willis Group Holdings, 137
Willis Tower, 137
Windows, best time to wash, 123–24
wine
   drink after uncorking, best time to, 154
   uncork, best time to, 153–154
work
   expect less fatigue, best time of day to,
     110–11
   get accomplished, best day of the week to,
     108–09

yacht, best time of year to buy and sell, 55

Zanzibar, best month to go, 144

BOOKS BY MARK DI VINCENZO

BUY SHOES ON WEDNESDAY AND TWEET AT 4:00
More of the Best Times to Buy This, Do That and Go There

ISBN 978-0-06-211770-0 (paperback)

Following the bestselling compendium *Buy Ketchup in May and Fly at Noon* comes another essential guide packed with expert tips. *Buy Shoes on Wednesday and Tweet at 4:00* covers an even wider range of topics and subjects, including sections on beauty, pets, cars, and children.

YOUR PINKIE IS MORE POWERFUL THAN YOUR THUMB
And 333 Other Surprising Facts That Will Make You Wealthier, Healthier and Smarter Than Everyone Else

ISBN 978-0-06-200835-0 (paperback)

Which is the most dangerous day of the year to drive a car? Why is 300 cents more than $3? Di Vincenzo has the answers along with more fascinating facts that are as much fun to pass on at the water cooler as they are useful.

BUY KETCHUP IN MAY AND FLY AT NOON
A Guide to the Best Time to Buy This, Do That and Go There

ISBN 978-0-06-173088-7 (paperback)

What's the best time of day to take your car in for an oil change? The best time of year to visit Rome? The best month to buy jeans? Get more for your money and maximize your time; take better care of your health and be savvier about your career—all by using Di Vincenzo's tips and tricks.